Warrior of Life

A Guide to Self-Transformation

Charles Householder

Householder Publishing Company
A Division of Householder Enterprises, Inc.

For information about special discounts for bulk purchases,
Please contact Householder Enterprises Sales at
http://www.charleshouseholder.com

Householder Jr., Charles K. (Charles Keith), 1974—
Warrior of Life: A Guide to Self-Transformation
1st edition

ISBN-13: 978-0-615-61663-6
ISBN-10: 0615616631

Acknowledgements

I am grateful for the many people who have played a positive role in my life by contributing in some way to my own personal growth and transformation. I have been blessed with many wonderful teachers, some of whom have been mentioned in this book. Thank you all! I promise to continue to share the wisdom you have bestowed upon me in grateful appreciation for all that I have received.

Writing this book was a labor of love for me. However, its completion is a result of the efforts of several people: my brother Anthony for willingly reading and editing the rough draft of this manuscript, and giving me guidance. My business partner Eric Meyer for his role in helping me to develop the manuscript, the artwork for the cover, and for partnering with me on getting this book to the people who can benefit from the information presented. Finally, Roger Templin for providing final edits of the book and helping me to express my ideas in a format that is concise and easy to understand.

Thank you to my parents Kathy and Chuck for raising me in a healthy and loving environment, providing me with support and guidance, and enabling me to do the things consistent with my dreams.

Thank you especially to my loving wife Sandra for your continued support, and for encouraging me to follow my excitement and live my purpose in this life.

Table of Contents

Introduction

This is a book about personal transformation and growth. The purpose of this book is to share with you my own pragmatic philosophy on creating success in all areas of life. The ideas, concepts, and strategies presented in this book are based on my over twenty years of collective research in mental and physical development, and spiritual refinement. This book will give you the tools to strengthen your mind, improve your health and fitness, connect with your spiritual source, and make a positive difference in the world. This will be done while showing you the most effective ways to set and achieve goals, overcome challenges, cultivate positive habits, identify and leverage personal resources, and persevere as you achieve the level of life success and happiness you desire.

I firmly believe that the purpose of life is growth, and if you are not growing you are dying. This of course isn't some cliché, but rather a fact of life. Nothing stays the same in nature. This means that in order to experience ongoing success you must continually be striving to get better and to grow in all the important areas of your life. A major part of success is choosing where you want to take your life and what you want to manifest. If you don't consciously make this choice, other factors will decide it for you, and your ultimate destination may not be somewhere you had ever wanted. This is essentially what was happening to me many years ago.

At a very young age, I found myself to be in a place where I felt total dissatisfaction with my life and my hopes for the future. I realized early on that I wasn't growing into the type of person I wanted to become. At that time in my life I was frustrated; I acted out in school and was a frequent target for bullies. I became cognizant that something had to change for me if my life was going to get better, and I understood that the only thing I had any control over actually changing was me. I am often amazed when I reflect back on my childhood and examine my behavior leading up to the point where I decided to change, for I can barely recognize the person I had been. It's often as if I am staring back at some other child rather than myself; however, that is the power of the personal transformation strategies presented in this book. In the next chapter, I will share more of this story. For now it is important for you to know that if you desire positive results in your life and are looking to grow, to become better today than yesterday, to make improvements in your health, your relationships, your work, or if you are just coasting along without a purpose in your life, and you endeavor to add some real meaning to it, you have come to the right place. This book will help you do just that. It sounds like a big promise; this I know. However, this book is based on actual practical application in my life and the life of the many students I have had the privilege to share this material with as a teacher and a coach through classes, seminars, and my Warrior of Life events over the past fifteen years.

Why the title "Warrior of Life?" "Warrior of Life" is a phrase I coined when I was twenty-one years old. I had the idea to teach a regular class on the martial arts to children of families who otherwise couldn't afford this type of training; yet, I wanted their training to be much more than the physical practice of self-defense techniques. I wanted them, through these classes, to gain the ability to deal with many of life's challenges, especially the challenges they were currently facing and those which lay ahead for them. Essentially, I wanted to share with them the type of holistic training I had for many years sought after myself. So, using the martial arts as a framework, I developed the Warrior of Life program. In these early classes, I shared with them mental development techniques, goal setting and achievement strategies, character building, problem solving, health and nutrition practices, and, of course, self-defense.

Since that first class over fifteen years ago, my own training experiences and knowledge have expanded far beyond what I ever could have imagined then, and so has my definition of a Warrior of Life.

The new definition and the aim of this book is to show individuals how to develop their own internal resources by strengthening their mind to overcome limiting beliefs, doubts, and fears; to strengthen their body and improve their health through the application of discipline and efficient effort; and to refine their spirit through active practices of gratitude, forgiveness, and a daily ritual of meditation and introspection. By turning their weaknesses into strengths and leveraging those strengths to overcome audaciously chosen challenges, to grow, and to achieve their goals, the Warrior of Life is then ready to take his most important steps which will contribute to his happiness and success, and that is by contributing to all of mankind in positive ways to make a major difference in the world.

To help readers live up to the preceding definition, the Warrior of Life book presents a holistic program for personal development and life success. The Warrior, whose definition conjures up images of discipline, persistence, strength, courage, and action serves as a worthy archetype consisting of positive characteristics for us to model as we undertake this life-changing program.

As the creator of this method for personal development, I devote the first chapter to sharing my own experiences and explaining how the material for this book came about. If someone is going to posit a "way," I believe they should clearly illustrate their credentials and experience, which is what most of the first chapter is devoted to. Also included in the first chapter is an overview of the aim of this book as well as a preview of some of the strategies that are going to be presented in the chapters that follow. The second chapter teaches the fundamental workings of the mind and how it is used to create our lives. The information presented in this chapter is derived from a combination of intense reading; personal instruction by various teachers spanning spirituality, religion, and metaphysical sciences; and, of course, the insights gleaned from my own personal experiences. Three fundamental techniques are next introduced in the third chapter which serves as a basis for immediately experiencing improvements in life. These techniques are intended to provide the flint to help ignite your internal fires and increase your thirst for the additional practical knowledge to be presented in the subsequent chapters. The first half of chapter four describes in detail many of my own experiences exploring the Spiritual component of life. The second half provides specific teachings and exercises to improve the mind and body en route to forming each individual's own spiritual practice. The Warrior of Life daily meditation, a core component of the program, is explained in detail and taught in this chapter. Chapters five and seven provide a unique process for learning and applying powerful mental techniques to significantly improve a person's life, by ultimately transforming their behaviors and helping them to effectively achieve their own specific goals. Using the martial arts ranking system as a framework, these chapters illustrate a practical method for advancing in mental power and applying these techniques immediately in our lives. In between these two chapters, the Warrior's clarity is developed and his targets are established through a very effective goal setting workshop. I have taught this goal setting workshop for several years now and it has proven to be one of the most helpful and effective processes for mapping one's life. Chapter eight combines many of the lessons already taught, along with cutting-edge information on nutrition and fitness. This unique approach presents an opportunity for individuals to leverage what's been learned in a way that will allow the budding Warrior of Life to make rapid and permanent behavioral changes that strengthen the physical body. If the reader has been applying what he has learned in a disciplined fashion, he will then be ready to make use of the number one strategy universally applied by all high achievers, what separates the winners in life as well as the Warrior of Life from the rest, which is presented in chapter nine. Chapter ten is the final chapter and is devoted to imparting the essential purpose of the Warrior, the underlying factor that lifts the Warrior's journey through life beyond the realm of mediocrity. The entire book has been designed as a practical pathway for all readers to grow through this program.

To get started, in the next few pages, you will be introduced to my own story, and you will discover what led to the insights you will learn through this book. Plus, you will come to understand how the Warrior of Life concept was conceived and how it grew from an idea, to this book, and into various other programs. The anecdotes presented in the next chapter and

4

throughout this book were written in such a way to illustrate the various success principles contained within the Warrior of Life program. Don't just read this book for entertainment, but seek to extract the principles contained therein, and endeavor to apply them in different ways immediately in your own life.

Chapter 1

Discovering the Way

My mother's first baby died a few hours after the baby had been born. My mom had carried the baby for nine months completely unaware that anything was wrong. Losing her child completely devastated my mom. Over the next few weeks and months she became more and more depressed. My father was afraid that she was having a nervous breakdown, since she was experiencing symptoms of anxiety, sadness, and hopelessness. She didn't seem to be getting any better, so he decided to visit their family physician for advice. The doctor's advice to my father was to hurry up and get her pregnant again. Nine months later I was born.

My parents Kathy and Chuck gave birth to a healthy nine and half pound baby boy. I was fortunate to have been born to two loving parents who were completely devoted to my well-being. However, even though I was completely healthy, my mother was terrified that something terrible was going to happen to me, as it had with her first child. This caused her to become more and more overprotective of me. For instance, when family and friends were visiting to see the newborn, my mom required them to wear a medical face mask to prevent the transmission of any germs. My mom has told me that when I was a child she was constantly watching over me, and, if I made the slightest sound, she would immediately coddle me.

As I became older, she grew more protective. For example, I lasted three days in nursery school, before she decided to keep me home until I had to enroll in kindergarten. My mom would let me play certain sports like other kids my age, but would typically err on the side of extreme caution when it came to allowing me to engage in most activities. Soon, without knowing it, I started to absorb many of the same fears my mother had for me, which kept me from engaging in activities typical for my age. I wouldn't play on the monkey bars or climb trees, for fear of falling. I wouldn't race or jump things on my bicycle, because I was afraid that I might get hurt. It is very obvious to me, now, that my mom's fear that something would happen to me was completely absorbed by my subconscious mind and manifested in my own behavior. As a result, throughout my childhood, whenever I got even slightly hurt, my first response was to run to the nearest adult and ask, "Am I going to die?"

Growing up, my younger brother and I spent most of our time with my mom and her sister, my aunt. My nearest male cousin was six years older, and, though I very much looked up to him, he wasn't around enough to have a measurable impact on forming my behavior. My father worked very hard, which allowed my mom to stay home with my brother and me. At the time, my father was building a career in the automotive industry, in which he started as salesperson and earned his way up to General Sales Manager. Unfortunately, his work demanded a lot of his time. During my childhood, he typically worked a sixty-hour week. At least three days each week, he worked twelve consecutive hours, and he worked every Saturday. Most days, I'd see him for a few minutes in the morning, and then again for a few minutes before bed at night. Even with all the hours he worked, my father would spend much of his free time with my brother and me; however, for me this proved to be insufficient to "toughen me up." I found myself, at the age of eleven, in the fifth grade, a small, fearful, whiny child. A boy with a litany of irrational fears, who, just as a lamp attracts flies, was a natural target for bullies.

My bully troubles began when I was in the fifth grade, but they weren't my only troubles. I knew that I wasn't like most other kids my age. I was very withdrawn, shy, fearful, and emotional – a polite way of saying whiny. I knew, even at that very young age, that it wasn't normal to be so frightened, but I didn't yet know how to change.

7

In our elementary school, the grades were from kindergarten to the sixth grade. Following sixth grade you graduated to the middle school, which was seventh and eighth grade, and then onto high school, which was grades nine through twelve. In our elementary school, the sixth graders were inspired into forming gangs by a charismatic young punk I'll call "Arnold Wesker". Arnold was small, but influential, and he surrounded himself with other larger kids and would naturally harass even smaller kids like me to build up his ego. In me, I can imagine, he saw an ideal target, someone, who was too small to fight back and perhaps too fearful to try. For most of my fifth grade experiences, this kid, along with his friends, constantly harassed me. It got so bad that I dreaded going to school. In fact, at one point, I had a rash on my body caused by stress and nervousness that actually kept me from going to school. My parents were very concerned and involved, taking actions, such as speaking to the principal and taking me to and from school. Unfortunately, they were overlooking the real source of my problems: me.

As I look back now, I am amazed that at such a young age I came to the following conclusion on my own. It was this perspective that laid the groundwork for me to completely change and improve my life, and throughout my life I have continued to reinforce the essence of this perspective in my mind. Here is that perspective: it dawned on me one day that I could not change the people that were bullying me. In fact, they were just doing what they were supposed to do. *They were bullies and I was a wimpy kid, and bullies harass wimpy kids.* If I wanted things to change, I was going to have to change the only thing that I could: myself. Once I came to this conclusion (or as I later learned in the teachings of Unity, a non-denominational Christian church, I had a "new thought"), my perspective shifted (this is key), and my world began to look brighter. I was done looking only at the problem; now, I was looking towards the solution—changing myself for the better.

Many years later I was introduced to the story of the Scorpion and the Frog. When I first heard this story, it made immediate sense to me because it reminded me of the conclusion I had come to when I was eleven. The story goes like this: One day there is a scorpion standing on a riverbank desiring to get to the other side. There the scorpion sees a frog floating on the river's surface and the scorpion asks the frog if he could ride on the frog's back to get to the opposite side. The frog responds to the scorpion saying absolutely not, that scorpions sting frogs, and if the frog lets the scorpion on his back, the scorpion will surely sting him, and he will die. The scorpion says to the frog that he won't sting him because if he did, then they would both die; the frog from the sting, and the scorpion from drowning. The frog thinks about it for a moment and, desiring to be helpful, agrees to allow the scorpion to climb on his back for passage to the other side. Half-way across the river the scorpion does in fact sting the frog. The frog is shocked! He says to the scorpion, "Why, why would you sting me? Yes I am going to die but now you are going to die too. Why would you sting me when in doing so you are killing yourself?"

To this the scorpion replies, "Because I am a scorpion and you are a frog and scorpions sting frogs."

The exact solution to my troubles came to me one Saturday afternoon while I was still in the fifth grade; I was inside the house, playing with my toy action figures, and the television was on in the background. While I was playing, a movie came on that was part of Saturday afternoon Kung Fu Theater. This movie caught my attention, as I watched a small, thin, Asian man defend himself against at least twenty other men. This Asian man was amazing; he threw kicks and punches with blinding speed, leaping, spinning and making quick work of every opponent. I will never forget that day, because it was at that moment, the solution to all of my problems presented itself--I would become a kung fu master. My whole mind accepted this thought immediately. It clearly resonated with me. I immediately ran to find and ask my mom to enroll me in kung fu/karate classes (I wasn't aware of the distinction yet). Little did I know, due to my mom's fear that I might get hurt and her belief that it would lead to more problems, such as fighting at school, it would take me two years before I was finally enrolled.

When I analyze this period of my life, there are two distinct observations that immediately stand out. The first is of the amazing gift of the imagination especially when it is put to use without limitations as is the case with young children. When I determined that becoming a kung fu master would solve my problems, I didn't doubt it. I didn't dwell on the time it might take, the obstacles I'd encounter, or even the unlikelihood that

9

this was even possible; instead, I kept imagining the possibility without limitation. This is a key to success in life! Don't limit your imagination, and, when you set a goal, any goal, let the visualization of that goal play out in your mind as if it were already achieved. Focus on the end result long enough and with enough intensity, and the steps to take will appear. This is a universal law, and has always been true in my own life.

The second observation is that once I made this my goal, my mind became attuned to it, and my reticular cortex was put into action. The reticular cortex is that part of the brain that, once you give it a goal, it goes into hyper-awareness, looking for anything associated with that goal. You'll often see this happening all the time in your own life. When you decide to buy a new car, for example, and you choose the type of car you want, you begin to notice that same type of car, model, and color everywhere you go. It's as if almost everyone in the entire world has become interested in the same car as you. What is really happening is that your mind is on the lookout for every manifestation of and approach to realizing your goal. Now that you are aware of this, put it to work for you. Once you set a goal, open your mind to the reality that opportunities are everywhere. Then be on the lookout as you go through your day, for people and resources that are available to help your achieve your desires.

When I entered the sixth grade, my bully problems subsided. The kids who had harassed me had moved onto the middle school, and I was given a reprieve. However, my goal was still the same, as was my urgency, since I knew that soon, I too, would graduate and move onto the middle school where the same group of kids who tormented me, or more, would be waiting.

During this time, I was seeing martial arts related items everywhere. When I went to the grocery store with my mom, I now saw that there were martial arts magazines for sale. When I flipped through the channels on TV, I now saw there were plenty of martial arts movies being played on television. Also, during this time, which was the mid-eighties, the ninja craze was sweeping America. I became infatuated with ninjas and decided to extend my goal beyond becoming a kung fu master to becoming a ninja. I decided that if I was a ninja, all my problems would be gone. I would be practically invincible, fearless, confident, and strong--all the things I clearly wasn't.

As I tried to formulate my plan, I was on the lookout for ninjutsu (martial art of the historic ninja) schools. Unfortunately, as I soon found out, none currently existed where I lived. I decided the first step of my plan would be to learn any good practical martial art, and, then, when the opportunity to become a ninja by learning ninjutsu presented itself, I would already have a strong foundation. *By the way, it eventually worked out something like this.* Later on while reflecting on this part of my life, the lesson I gleaned from this experience was that the more regularly I focused on my desire, the more a clear plan for manifesting it began to emerge. This is also universally true. *The more clarity you have regarding your desire through frequent contemplation of it, the quicker a plan begins to present itself for you to act upon.*

However, at this time in my life, my mom still wasn't budging and wouldn't enroll me in the martial arts. This didn't deter me, though; I remained steadfast in my determination, each day visualizing what my life would be like once I had reached my goal. I kept doing this because the visualization felt good. It felt better than my current reality, which is why I would focus on it so much (another key to achievement).

As I look back, it appears so obvious the way things unfolded to help me on my own personal journey, but, of course, there was no way to tell this at the time. During the summer between sixth and seventh grade, I was dreading going to the middle school. Also, I thought I was still no physically closer to learning the martial arts. I hadn't even picked out a specific school yet; I just knew my goal. Then, in the end of June, my mom and aunt took my brother and me to a festival the next town over. There, a local martial arts school The Ansonia Tae Kwon Do Academy was giving a demonstration in the afternoon. I begged my mom to let us stay since I had never seen a live martial arts demonstration before, and she agreed.

The demonstration was amazing. I saw kids of all ages performing self-defense movements, using martial arts weapons, rolling and flipping, and breaking boards. These guys moved like the ninjas portrayed in movies. I immediately wanted to go to that school and learn to do what I saw these people doing. However, my mom still didn't want to enroll me in martial arts, and she encouraged me to do other activities like baseball and soccer. In my mind, all I could think about was going to this school.

Turning Point

Seventh grade started off just as I had feared. My bully troubles picked up right where they had left off, and this inspired me to even more intensely think about my goal; nevertheless, it still seemed to me that I wasn't getting any closer to experiencing it in my reality. Luckily, the Universe had other plans.

One day in mid-November, Arnold, who had once again been harassing me more often (this time backed by a group of kids who were as big as fully grown adults, with one kid who could grow a full beard), sat next to me on the school bus. I typically sat in the first few seats on the bus, and, when he rode the bus, which was infrequently, he sat with the "cooler" kids in the back. As the bus got within a few minutes of my stop, he sat next to me, and, to my surprise, he was talking in a pretty friendly manner to me. Little did I know that he was biding his time in order to pull off a nefarious act. Unbeknownst to me, in his far hand was a dollop of shaving or moisturizing cream. As we pulled up to my stop, he stood up, smacked the cream into my head, and said something like, "So long punk."

As I stood up and looked at him I had no idea what had just happened, until I saw the rest of the kids laughing at me. I reached up and could feel the cream in my hair. I started yelling back at him but felt helpless to do anything. He was in the back of the bus among his friends; we were at my stop, and the bus driver, who was unaware of what had just taken place, was waiting for me to exit the school bus. I got off the bus, still trying to put on a brave face, yelling swears and names back at him in anger, but, as the bus drove away, I felt sad and humiliated.

A few moments later, I walked in the front door of our house where my mom was waiting for me at the top of the stairs. She asked me how my day was but saw from my body language that something was wrong. I burst out crying, and she came down to try to comfort me. I don't remember anything that was actually said during our brief conversation, except for the last thing she said, which sounded almost frantic, as she, too, had started to cry. The words that she said were "What do you want me to do?" To which I replied, "Sign me up for karate!"

And then it happened, the Universe had delivered to me the catalyst to achieve my vision, along with plenty of negative experiences, which I reframed into reasons to follow through, once I'd begun. My mom, who cared for her children more than anything, finally got that I desperately needed this, and, the following week, I was enrolled at the Ansonia Tae Kwon Do Academy.

Preparation

People are attracted to the martial arts for a variety of reasons and at different times in their lives. Some do it as a fun activity or as a regular hobby; some enroll to get in better physical shape; others do it to learn self-defense, to handle bullies, or even to confront worse situations, e.g. law enforcement training. For me, learning the martial arts was intended to be the vehicle I needed to change my life.

As you will learn again later in this book, a vehicle is a great metaphor for achievement. I had a vision and I had goals, but the vehicle (the martial arts) enabled me to take the fast lane toward achieving my goals and realizing the vision I had for my life. Martial arts aren't the only vehicles, but every good vehicle to success should have the following characteristics. The first is a coach or mentor. The starting point of all notable achievement beyond just the martial arts is almost always to find a good coach or mentor. In Japanese, the title for the head of a martial arts school is sensei with translates to mean the one who has gone before. In other words, the sensei knows the way because he has traveled the road before. He can guide you and coach you. Also, because he has accomplished what you are choosing to accomplish, your association with a good coach reinforces the belief that your goal is possible for you. At the Ansonia Tae Kwon Do Academy I had been blessed with an amazing coach, Master Mike Trimarchi, to guide me on my journey.

The second thing is the passengers who are along for the ride with you. There is much truth to the statement, *you become like the people you hang around with*. Hanging around with like-minded individuals who will push you, challenge you, and help you to succeed is extremely valuable. In fact, a determinant of success can be found in examining who are you hanging around with, and what they are doing to you. Fortunately for me, some of the best people I have ever met and associated with regularly were devoted students of the martial arts.

For me, martial arts training wasn't a hobby or an activity, but rather it was to be the vehicle by which I would change my life. Now that I was enrolled, I established new goals to serve as benchmarks along the way. The first goal I committed myself to was to earn my black belt. The next goal was to become a martial arts instructor. I also envisioned that if I were as skilled as Master Trimarchi, the head instructor of the Ansonia Tae Kwon Do Academy, then I would have manifested the vision of the person I intended to become with all the matching characteristics. In addition to his acting as both my Instructor and my coach, eventually, I also began modeling my own performance after his, as well as after the ability of his senior students in order to improve myself more quickly.

Before the first class, I did something that I didn't come to recognize as being a formal personal development practice, until I read about it many years later in a personal growth book. I started establishing new *rules* for myself and for how I was going to behave. Later, I learned that establishing rules for our behavior is something that we often do unconsciously as part of the socialization process. In my case, setting new rules for my behavior seemed like a great idea since I was beginning on a brand new journey, which I was certain would have a profound positive impact on my life.

Determining that the first martial arts class would serve as the official beginning of my pursuit to a changed life, I started developing a set of rules for my conduct and began employing them that very first class. As I made more decisions, I added to my list of rules. Eventually, the rules became a part of my being, and I no longer had to think about them. They were habitual. Here are some of the rules I made for myself back then:

1. I would do everything my instructor suggested for my improvement (no-brainer).
2. I would practice incessantly, including and especially, the days that I didn't have class.
3. I would no longer whine or cry; I would never cry due to physical pain.
4. If I fell down, I would immediately bounce back to my feet.
5. I would never quit.
6. I would always stand up for myself and for others (Chuck Norris inspired this rule).

Over twenty years later, I still practice the martial arts incessantly. I am extremely positive; I look for solutions; I don't get deterred and, funnily enough, I have an amazingly high pain tolerance. My pain tolerance is so high that, on two occasions, medical doctors had a difficult time diagnosing a serious injury I had sustained, because I didn't exhibit the typical pain symptoms. I believe this is more of a result of twenty years of mental conditioning and state management than a biological occurrence.

Personal Transformation

Finally, after two years of waiting, I arrived to take my very first martial arts lesson. I still can recall vividly that very first class. I was like a sponge absorbing everything I was being shown, modeling the instructor, and taking in with all of my senses everything going on around me. I was filled with excitement and enthusiasm, and that night I went to bed with a feeling of assurance that I was heading in the right direction, and things were going to be different for me.

Within just a few weeks, my martial arts practice was starting to have an impact on me, and my confidence was steadily increasing. This must have shown up in my total appearance, because, without any additional effort on my part, my bully problems just started to fade away. Arnold seemed to lose interest, which makes sense from a metaphysical perspective, since he had *served his role in my transformation and was no longer required.* (A great way to look at all the challenges in your life is as if they are serving a role to help you grow, improve, and succeed.) The other bullies stopped bothering with me as well. Plus, now, I had a purpose each day and that was this: to continue to absorb and practice the martial arts driven self-development program I was creating for myself. This sense of purpose was also having a measurable positive impact on my attitude and behavior. I looked forward to going to school now; I was excited about going to martial arts classes afterwards and then sharing the unique skills I was learning with my family and friends.

The martial arts played a major role in my total life transformation; however, even though I didn't realize this on a conscious level, deeper in my mind (my subconscious), I knew that it wasn't quite enough. This is why I believe I was led to the next big discovery in my life. This discovery opened doors for me to greater life skills and abilities consistent with my vision for my future. Here is how it came about:

I had only been practicing the martial arts for five or six months. I was thirteen years old and in the seventh grade. It was a Sunday afternoon and my father had been out running errands in the morning. (You should know that my father is an avid golfer and has always been committed to improving his game. At the current time I write this, he is one of the top golfers at his club.) That early Sunday afternoon, when my father returned home, he told me that he had been at the bookstore at the local mall, looking for golf books, and he discovered, on the same shelf, a handful of books teaching different styles and aspects of the martial arts. Up to his point it hadn't really dawned on me that there were books like this that might be this readily available. I excitedly requested he take me there immediately, and, a short while later, I was scanning the titles of books on the shelf at that very bookstore. The book that practically jumped out at me was a book called Mystic Arts of the Ninja by American Ninjutsu Master Stephen K. Hayes. This was my first martial arts book and I still have it in my personal library, over twenty years later, only, now, it has been personally autographed by the Ninjutsu Master himself. This book was a combination of a ninja history lesson, along with techniques on hand-to-hand combat, use of the sword, short stick and throwing star (common ninja weapons), as well as the esoteric spiritual practices of the ninja. Needless to say, I was blown away. I must have read and practiced the techniques in the book thousands of times. Eventually, I had the pleasure of meeting Master Hayes while attending a seminar he was giving. He is even more amazing in person as he appeared to be in the eyes of an enthusiastic young boy poring over his books.

It is rare, if not impossible, for a neophyte to learn a martial art by reading a book; however, for a practicing martial artist to enhance his or her training by using books, it is both common and effective. Each time I went to the mall with my parents, I would fast-track it to the bookstore looking for new martial arts books. I would buy the books that most interested me, go home, and practice what the book taught. Then, I would bring the skills with me to the dojang (Korean term for martial arts training hall) to see if I could make them work during actual training.

Then, on one particular evening a few years later--I suspect I was about sixteen--I was in a bookstore, and, after scanning the titles of martial arts books and not seeing anything new and interesting that I hadn't already read, I decided to explore the rest of the store. That is when I wandered over to the self-help section and made the discovery that would have a major impact in changing my life.

Since you've been reading this far you can understand how I might have needed a few more tools to become the person possessing all the positive qualities I desired. With this in mind, as I scanned the shelf, the self-help section titles started to jump out at me, and I felt the same excitement I first felt when I was introduced to the martial arts books. Books like *How to Win Friends and Influence People*, *The Magic of Thinking Big*, *Think and Grow Rich*, and *The Ultimate Secrets of Total Self Confidence* immediately caught my attention. That night, I purchased *How to Win Friends and Influence People*, by Dale Carnegie, and also *The Ultimate Secrets of Total Self Confidence*, by Dr. Robert Anthony, and these two books started me off on a program of reading for personal development that has never stopped. Since that day, I have read over a thousand books on self-help, business, health, psychology, religion, and the martial arts. My personal library at home boasts of over five hundred of my favorite books, which I continue to read and re-read as I mentally program myself for continued, never-ending improvement and achievement in life. Together, the physical practice of martial arts, combined with the mental habit of reading non-fiction books geared towards success, are two of the three pillars that formed the foundation for my total life transformation back in my early to mid-teen years.

It took me five years of dedicated practice to earn the coveted black belt. Earning my black belt was one of my proudest achievements. One of the many benefits I derived from this undertaking was learning how to accomplish a long term goal. Five years is a long time, and being able to commit myself to this undertaking, which required considerable devotion and the ability to circumnavigate obstacles, has instilled in me the virtue of persistence. During this five year period, I was constantly refining my behavior, my thinking, and my character. For example, I would look for characteristics I admired in other people, such as my instructor, my peers, people I read about in biographical books and magazines, as well as heroic individuals portrayed on TV. When I saw a characteristic I admired, I would model the individual characteristic and then practice the corresponding behavior in my daily life. This was a conscious practice of identifying and modeling individual behaviors, until eventually it became a natural part of my conduct. I have many success stories on how well this worked, as well as humorous anecdotes from that period of my life, one in particular that depicts a less than positive ramification.

Around that time in my life I had watched a western with my Dad featuring Clint Eastwood. The silent cowboy, tough guy type Eastwood portrayed appealed to me. I wanted to incorporate those characteristics into my behavior, and I thought the best way to get the feeling of being Eastwood's character and absorbing his character's behaviors was to practice his squint. I would go through my day practicing my Eastwood squint. I'd employ it during martial arts practice to intimidate my opponents. Later on, this squint became part of a behavioral anchor I would engage in to get into a resourceful state of mind before a competition. The less than positive ramification I was referring to is that I believe this practice led to my needing corrective lenses to remedy the nearsightedness which began shortly thereafter.

There is a saying in the martial arts that goes, "you attract the teacher you deserve." I think this is the martial arts approach of illustrating the Law of Attraction in action. I was very fortunate to attract into my life Mike Trimarchi. His positive impact on my life still shows up in my behavior and corresponding actions. He began studying the martial arts while living in California. His Korean Tae Kwon Do instructor, Chong Lee, was a world-renowned expert on the art of kicking and had authored several books on the subject. Mike studied with Chong Lee, eventually earning his black belt, and then returned to Connecticut, where he expanded his training to include other martial arts. Currently, he is a sixth degree master of the martial arts. He is an amazing instructor, totally committed to his student's development. As a person, he is very humble, considering the amazing achievements he has made in his life and the martial arts. For instance, even though he has attained a high rank in the martial arts and operated his own successful martial arts school for over 30 years, he has always been very open to learning other martial arts skills and from other qualified practitioners. I remember how he would always welcome into his school other instructors who had something of value to teach, and he would work hard to incorporate those skills into his repertoire. As a result, he created a system of martial arts that is both eclectic and holistic. It was holistic, meaning that, as his students, we learned kicking, boxing, grappling, throwing, ground fighting, weapons, and rolling (to name just a few styles); he was teaching "mixed martial arts" before there was ever a name for it. Essentially, he has always been focused on developing the total martial artist, and, even though Tae Kwon Do served as a great foundation, he encouraged his students, by his example, to continue to enhance their skills by learning other disciplines and applying what was practical.

His approach to the martial arts resonated with me. It was similar to the approach I was taking to improving my life. By studying multiple disciplines and applying what was useful to my own life, I had been able to create a measurable improvement in my thinking, my attitude, my behavior, my health, and my character. After earning my black belt, I continued to train with Master Trimarchi, but I now began looking for and studying other martial arts. I demonstrated the same level of humility and respect that I had seen him exhibit, and this opened doors for me to amazing instructors and unique systems.

By my senior year of high school, I was a black belt in the martial arts, and I had been training regularly with a handful of talented martial arts instructors. At this point, I still had a list of personal development goals I was working on and a hazy vision of what I was going to do after high school. Luckily, after a brief conversation with my father one afternoon, a path appeared to me which eventually led to defining the direction for the rest of my life. My father asked me one day what I was planning to do after I graduated. I told him that I was going to open up my own martial arts school. He replied by asking me where I intended to get the money.

Not having really thought about it, I responded that I was hoping to get it from him, to which he said that he didn't have the money set aside to give me, but he had spoken to a friend of his who was an executive at a local manufacturing facility, and this friend was willing to give me a job on the assembly line once I finished high school. The thought of spending my life on the assembly line didn't appeal to the expanded vision I was just starting to create for my life, and this was just the motivation I needed to make the decision to enroll in college to enhance my skills and broaden my knowledge. While I was in college, Master Trimarchi helped me to get started running my own martial arts school by helping me to create a program at the local YMCA. There, I operated my own school that catered to both children and adults. Even though I thoroughly enjoyed teaching the martial arts, and I had achieved the second benchmark goal I had set for myself when I first started training which was to become an Instructor, I had this expanding feeling inside me that there was something more that I wanted to do in my life.

I spent the following summer intensely practicing the martial arts, which included travelling to Los Angeles, California to learn jiu-jitsu at a seminar at the world famous Gracie Academy. There I met Rob Kahn (who later went on to become Royce Gracie's first black belt), who had been at the Gracie Academy for several months training and was returning to his home in Westchester, New York around the same time I was coming back to Connecticut. I invited Rob to come teach us at the Ansonia Tae Kwon Do Academy, which he accepted, and thus began my love affair with the martial art of Brazilian Jiu-jitsu. My plan for the fall semester at college was to take a full course load, teach martial arts three days a week, and continue to practice jiu-jitsu during my other free time. Then, something happened next that would have a profound impact on me and help me to put my future in perspective.

Wake Up Call

On a Monday afternoon in the beginning of September, I was involved in a head-on car collision that, fortunately, only left me with a badly broken nose. The car was totaled; the windshield was cracked; I hadn't been wearing a seat-belt, and even though I needed surgery to rebuild my nose, I had escaped the accident pretty much physically intact. Mentally, however, it was a different case. The reality that my life could have ended right there, on that highway, on a Monday afternoon, was a wake-up call that, even then, I didn't realize would have a major affect on my life. This realization was one that would leave an indelible mark on my psyche for a long time to come, and it would set me down the path to creating an enhanced vision for my life, which ultimately led to developing the Warrior of Life program.

I say the accident served as a "wake up call" for me because, even though my life seemed to be traveling in the direction I wanted, I had started to grow complacent enjoying my earlier successes, without expanding the plans I had for my future. After the car accident, I started to appreciate how transitory life is, and this discovery infused me with a newfound sense of urgency, which I used to propel me forward again, towards a larger vision and new goals. I came to the realization that, even though I enjoyed teaching the martial arts, I wanted to have an even greater impact on people's lives. I wanted to make a larger difference in how well a person's life turned out, and I wanted to reach more people beyond only those interested in learning a martial art.

The basic challenges and demands of daily life started to become more apparent to me now, and, at the same time, this contributed to an idea I had of creating a framework which would help those, who applied it, to surmount any obstacle in their way, en route to the life of their dreams. I knew that I wasn't yet prepared to create this framework or to share this philosophy with other people, so I committed myself to this larger vision for my future. My new strategy would be to advance my own personal self-development program which had been unfolding for the past ten years, by measuring the progress I had made through various tests, while simultaneously expanding my studies on achieving success in life, by investigating other methodologies and philosophies.

Also, as a result of the car accident and the subsequent introspection, I recognized a part of my life that had been missing up to this point, and that was the spiritual component. I have always believed that we are all spiritual beings having a human experience, and I recognized that I had only been paying casual attention to this important part of my being. This inspired me to set the new intention to focus on developing my spiritual practice which was to essentially build a closer relationship with my Creator, who I also call Source, and God.

Once I had made these two decisions (1. to expand my study of life-success while testing my progress and to create a framework for others to use to succeed, and 2. develop a relationship with my Source), new opportunities for personal growth began to appear. I discovered a Buddhist temple, which was located on the route I had been driving each day to school. A relative of one of my students showed up in class one day and turned out to be a Yoga Instructor from Arizona, who agreed to give me private yoga instruction in exchange for martial arts training. While glancing at a newspaper sitting on the treadmill next to mine in the gym, I came across an article on a local Reiki Master in New Haven who was giving instruction. These and many other opportunities like them continued to unfold in my life. Eventually, over the next ten years, while building a successful career in sales and sales management, with the intention of someday teaching these business skills to help contribute to a person's economic success, I studied and practiced everything I could find that would advance my goals. In addition to studying success through books and seminars, I sought out experiences such as skydiving, walking on fire, running a marathon, deep water scuba-diving, sweat lodges, and rock climbing to apply what I was learning and to test my new attitudes and skills. Also, during that course of time, I read over a thousand books; I became certified to teach several martial arts; I became a Reiki Master; I regularly practiced Tibetan Dzogchen Buddhism. I participated in several traditional Native American ceremonies, including an intense vision quest; I studied Chi-Gung, Taoism, and other energy systems; I taught yoga. I attended seminars led by business leaders like Brian Tracy, Zig Ziglar, and Jim Cathcart; by martial arts masters like Stephen K. Hayes, Rorion and Royce Gracie, and the late Soke (Japanese term for Grandmaster) Glen Morris; and by spiritual teachers like Wayne Dyer. I continued to test myself and expand my achievements by earning my skydiving license, becoming certified in SCUBA and scuba-diving all over the Atlantic Coast and the Caribbean, taking flying lessons, and participating in all types of endurance events.

All along the way, I continually had one thing in mind, which was to synthesize all of these experiences into a practical approach to authentic successful living supported by results. By journaling all of the teachings I was immersing myself in, along with my own personal insights and anecdotes, today, I have a volume of fifteen personal journals chronicling much of what I had been exposed to throughout this part of my life. In a crude fashion, to quickly delineate between what would work and what didn't, I would make a crass comparison between a winner and a loser, rich and poor, and the successful versus unsuccessful person when making notes in my journals. Eventually, I started to see similarities in the core thinking and behaviors of the winner, the rich, and the successful. These similarities I grouped together into what would be some of the core criteria for becoming a Warrior of Life, using the archetype of a warrior as the model for success.

This book is a result of all of that study and application. In the next chapter you will be introduced to the fundamental workings of our material universe. This information has been distilled into its simplest form, derived from the hundreds of books, seminars, and classes I have attended in order to come to know and understand this information.

Action Steps:

1. What are some circumstances or areas in your life that you would like to change? Write these down.
2. Look at what you wrote, and identify ways in which you may have been shifting the blame to something, or someone, outside of yourself.
3. Next, ask yourself, "What about you needs to change before your circumstances can change?"
4. Write down what these changes will look like (get ready to learn how to make them happen).
5. Examine who you are hanging around with. What are these associations doing to you? Decide to spend more time with the people who are having a positive effect on your behavior.

Chapter 2

Manifesting Life Success

It is not well known, outside of the martial arts, which system of fighting Bruce Lee originally studied before going on, to form his own system and to achieve movie fame. The very first style of fighting Bruce Lee learned which had a significant impact on his own style was the system of Wing Chun Kung Fu. One legend tells us that Wing Chun is a relatively new system developed by a female nun of the Shaolin Temple, and a master of Shaolin Kung Fu, only about three hundred years ago. She developed this system to enable her, not only to defend herself as a petite woman up against larger men, but also to defeat all other fighting styles she might encounter. Wing Chun interestingly is referred to by some of the masters I have met as the "anti-martial art". Several years ago, the opportunity presented itself for me to begin an intense study of Wing Chun with two local masters who were in the process of launching their own kwoon (Chinese word for school). In my very first lesson, I learned the basic mechanics of a powerful technique, which was, by the way, a favorite of Bruce Lee. This technique is commonly referred to in English as the "straight blast". The straight blast is a continuous series of rhythmic punches designed to overwhelm and overpower the opponent to the point where he can no longer prevent the onslaught of punches to his face and chest. My Sifu (Chinese word for instructor) explained to me that the straight blast is the core technique in this system, and everything else I learned, and would learn, for the most part was designed to get me in a position to make full use of the straight blast.

Just like in the preceding example, where an entire system of self-defense was centered around a core technique, as you will learn, every technique that has been created for the purpose of manifesting success is based on a fundamental law of the universe. In fact, at its focal point, every effective self-growth methodology is just another way of attuning your mind to make further use of the forthcoming concept. For instance, some success achievement methods may include writing and re-writing goals, verbalizing affirmations, scheduling visualization sessions or creating vision boards, acting as if, or replacing limiting beliefs. All of these methods are powerful; they all work, and many will be further explained in this book. However, please realize that each method is designed to make use of the forthcoming fundamental principle for life success; a fundamental concept underlying all of creation in the universe, which is this: *your thoughts become things*. This can be said another way as "what you think about comes about."

Your Thoughts Become Things

Our thoughts have tremendous power. Everything you can be, do, or have first begins with a thought; therefore, every thought matters. They influence our attitudes, our expectations, and our actions. By influencing our actions, our thoughts determine what we are able to manifest in the world. In addition, the thoughts we think contribute to our view of the world and how we choose to experience the events and circumstances in our lives. As Shakespeare has said, "There is nothing either good or bad, but thinking makes it so." Furthermore, our thoughts determine what stimuli in our environment we pay attention to and those which we ignore, what opportunities we notice and which opportunities end up passing us by.

Cumulative Power of Thought

Our thoughts can be classified as either positive or negative. Thoughts that are consistent with what we want, or would like to see happen, and that feel good, are typically positive. Thoughts that make up our fears, our worries,

26

and our concerns, and don't feel good are almost always negative. Thoughts have a cumulative power as well. You start with one thought that is either positive or negative, and it attracts additional thoughts of the same kind. In this way, our thoughts act like a magnet, attracting more and more of the same. I am sure you have experienced this phenomenon in your life, as well. For example, something seemingly bad may happen that is inconsequential, such as temporarily losing your car keys, but by focusing on the bad, your mind continues to find more and more like thoughts, and before you know it, you're thinking how your life is in shambles, and nothing seems to ever go right, all because you temporarily misplaced your car keys. Fortunately, the opposite is true as well. Start thinking of all the things that are going good in your life, and your mind will supply more and more good things to think about. This aspect can be referred to as the *cumulative power of thought.*

The cumulative power of thought can be continually leveraged by you, each day of your life, to improve your attitude. A great way to begin making use of this power is to start each day by thinking about your blessings. List in your mind or vocalize, all of the things in your life that you are grateful for. The famous motivational speaker Zig Ziglar has shared the following advice which states plainly, the practical value contained in this practice: "The more things you give thanks for, the more you will receive to be thankful for." This is a great practice to orient your day in a positive direction, and it is something we will look at, in more detail, in chapter four.

Law of Attraction

Like everything else in the universe, our thoughts are made up of energy. As energy, the thoughts we think have a vibratory quality. For this reason, in addition to labeling the nature of our thoughts as positive or negative, we can also classify them as strong or weak, as it relates to their vibration. Strong feeling thoughts, regardless of whether or not they are positive or negative, are the most powerful and have the greatest effect on our behavior, as well as what we attract into our lives.

As if by magic, the thoughts which originate in our mind travel out into the universe, pulling the objects and situations that most closely match up with the vibration of those thoughts, back into our experience. This phenomenon is commonly referred to as The Law of Attraction. The Law of Attraction is often described as the fundamental law of the universe. This law essentially states that we attract everyone, and everything, into our lives by the thoughts that we think. An important thing to note is that we are constantly attracting. This law is ALWAYS in effect. Every single thought counts. The Law of Attraction responds to your positive thoughts by bringing into your life things that you desire, just as easily as it responds to your negative thoughts, attracting those things you can do without. The Law of Attraction is impartial; it doesn't reason; it simply responds to the thoughts you are entertaining. Whatever you focus your mind on you will eventually see manifested in some form in your environment. In this way, the Law of Attraction acts like the Genie in Aladdin's lamp, forever responding to your thoughts with the phrase, "your wish is my command."

If you think the desire, "I want to be a millionaire," the Law of Attraction responds with "your wish is my command," and begins to attract objects and opportunities into your life consistent with your thought; however, if your next thought is, "but I could never earn that much money," the Law of Attraction responds "your wish my command," and you essentially cut yourself off from your initial desire.

The most important thing to always realize is that your thoughts are in your control. You might not actually believe that, though, if the majority of your thoughts up to now have been negative and focused on the opposite of what you want. In fact, I have come to realize that most people don't take any control over their thoughts, and they allow their minds to dwell upon the very things that they don't want, thereby attracting more thoughts of the same and eventually bringing those things into their life experience. Worry is an example of this. Worry can also easily be called "negative goal setting," for when we worry we are focusing on and thereby attracting the very things we don't want.

Thought Control

The fundamental and most practical skill for success in life is simply learning to control and direct our thoughts. Of course, for the majority of people, this is easier said than done.

There are three main ways in which I teach people how to begin controlling their thoughts and directing them, towards their goals and the things they want, and away from things they don't want:

The first method is to begin paying attention to the way that you feel. What to me sounds mystical, but in reality for all of us is commonplace, is that we all can feel the vibration and nature of our thoughts, simply, by paying attention to our emotions and how we are feeling, when we are thinking a particular thought. Almost always, our feelings and emotions are an exact match to the type of thoughts we are currently thinking in that moment. The thoughts that feel the best, and are the strongest, are typically the ones most consistent with our desires and the things we actually want. On the other hand, if you're feeling bad, and you examine the thought underlying that feeling, you would typically find that you're dwelling on some type of negativity which is contributing to those bad feelings. By frequently paying attention to your feelings, you will begin to discover the underlying cause contributing to those feelings, and, then, if it is a thought you don't want, simply by an act of your conscious mind, you can change it, by substituting a better one. The key is to condition yourself to pay attention to your feelings on a regular basis, and to make negative feelings a trigger, designed to cause you to make a conscious mental change of what you are thinking in that moment. The easiest way to change a negative thought is to identify its opposite, which should represent what you would prefer. So whenever you feel bad, use this as a trigger (a trigger is anything that serves as a stimulus and initiates or precipitates a reaction, or series of reactions) to immediately identify the thought you are thinking and change it to a positive thought. Make it a must to continually entertain in your mind, positive thoughts that feel good.

The second method is to pay attention to the things you say, specifically if those things are negative, such as when you are complaining. Since our words are a manifestation of our thoughts, whenever we are complaining, we are thinking and speaking about that which we don't want. If we continue to think about and speak about the things we don't want, eventually, those things, or their essence, will manifest in our reality. The best thing you can do is to pay attention to the various times you may find yourself complaining. When you catch yourself, immediately stop, and then change that thought. Begin speaking about what is it you want to

29

experience instead. A while ago, I read about a program that offered a similar approach to what I was teaching, but it combined a tangible method for making it workable in people's lives. The program was created by a Unity Church minster and is called, "A Complaint Free World." In this program, you are encouraged to purchase a bracelet to wear, and, each time you catch yourself vocalizing a complaint, you switch the bracelet to the other wrist. The goal is to go 21 days without vocalizing a complaint, and, therefore, without having to switch the bracelet. This is a great way to condition your thoughts and to program your mind for success. You can purchase your own bracelet at http://www.acomplaintfreeworld.org

Proactively, you can also use the power of the spoken word to fill your mind with positive thoughts, by taking time throughout each day to affirm the very things you would like to see appearing in your life. Positive affirmations are a very powerful tool for focusing your subconscious mind on your goals, as well as effecting a positive change in your attitude and behavior. I will talk more about affirmations and positive self-talk in this book. For now, begin noticing whenever you say something about yourself that you don't want to be true. When you catch yourself doing this, stop, change it, and then repeat the statement that you desire to be true for you in your life.

The third way to begin controlling your thoughts, and thereby your mind, is to consciously give yourself something specific to think about, and the best thing to be thinking about are those things which you desire. The best way to do this is to actively choose what it is you want to experience now, or, at least, sometime in your future. This essentially creates a vision for your future, which you can think about often. This becomes a proactive way to orient your mind in the direction you want your life to travel. Plus, since we have learned that the thoughts we think become things, if we think about what we desire, this will go a long way in helping us to manifest these things in our physical reality.

Long Term Thinking

As I look back at my life I often find it remarkable how, at such a young age, I was already beginning to imagine the type of life that I wanted to have, by the time I was eighteen and finished with high school. By determining exactly the vision that I wanted for myself, I was able to make significant changes in my life. By dwelling on this vision each and every day with such strong positive emotions, I was able to make the Law of Attraction work for me, by allowing it to bring to me the people, things, and circumstances consistent with my vision.

The most important thing to remember is that whenever you are thinking about your future you must be thinking positively and optimistically. As you already know from reading my condensed biography in the first chapter, I had little or no reason to mentally reinforce the vision I had for myself filled with the qualities I wanted to cultivate. At that time I was a weak and whiny child and the complete opposite of the person I wanted to become. Plus, I was surrounded by adults, who, like most people, typically held the belief that people didn't change. Even though they may not have been speaking about me, these were the beliefs I had to overcome in my own life. What I discovered is, the more I kept focusing on the vision, the clearer it became, and without analyzing my beliefs or assessing my resources, I was soon noticing that things were happening in my life, which, eventually, allowed me to manifest that early vision into my physical experience.

Developing a vision for your life is synonymous with "Long term positive thinking". Long term positive thinking is a hallmark of successful individuals. Instead of letting life act upon them, these people, through the power of their own thinking, become an active, creative participant in their own lives. The scale between success and failure can often be measured on the basis of long term positive thinking. On the success end of the scale are those people who are planning their lives and their company's, twenty or more years into the future. Diametrically opposed, residing on the complete other end of the spectrum, would be someone who is thinking only a few moments into the future, like that junkie focusing on where to get his next fix.

Starting from the failure end of the scale, which is measured by thinking in hours, you get to the next individual, who is thinking a day to a week ahead. This person may be living paycheck to paycheck, in a downward spiral, that won't change until he changes. The only way he can change is by starting with a change in his thinking. This I mentioned earlier, and it is completely under his own control. Further along, there might be an individual who is thinking a year, or even three years ahead, but he isn't thinking of a positive vision to manifest, so, instead, he may be thinking of potential problems on the horizon. Little does he know, the more he focuses on the problem, the greater his chances to eventually manifest it in his life, because of the Law of Attraction.

Subconscious Mind

Fortunately, we humans have all been blessed with a very powerful mechanism of mind that is designed for our survival, which can also be utilized to make us flourish. This mechanism is a component of the part of the mind referred to as our subconscious. Countless books have been written about the power of the subconscious and how to make use of it in our daily lives. The subconscious is the part of the mind that exists beyond consciousness, and it is responsible for all the automatic physiological process taking place beneath our conscious awareness. The domain of the subconscious mind also includes mental processes, and it is the seat of faculties such as the intuition, hunches, and problem solving. As a result of these faculties, the subconscious can be described as solution-oriented. For example, give the subconscious a problem to solve, and soon the solution will be presented to your conscious (reasoning) mind typically in the form of a hunch, or intuitive impulse upon which to act. All of us are blessed with a solution-oriented survival mechanism represented by the subconscious faculty of the mind. However, the majority of people don't utilize it on purpose, or on a regular basis. Nevertheless, there are multiple ways in which we can put our subconscious mind to work in our lives, and we can thereby enjoy many powerful benefits. Here are two, which you can begin using immediately:

The first way to enlist the aid of our subconscious mind to assist us in our life is to give it a problem to solve, and the best way to do this is to pose the problem as a question. The subconscious mind can answer any question that is presented to it in the proper way. From my research, I have discovered that there are certain methods that produce the best results when trying to gain the help of the subconscious mind in answering a question (solving a problem). The first is to pose the question when the subconscious is most amenable, such as right before you go to sleep at night. Oftentimes, many people will remark how they went to bed with a challenge on their mind, and when they woke up, they had a solution. This is an example of the subconscious mind in action. Another way is to write the question at the top of a page, and then to relax and write down as many possible solutions as come to mind (relaxing makes the subconscious more accessible). Encourage yourself to come up with twenty. If you do this, typically contained within those twenty is the best solution to the question. These are two powerful ways to solve any problems in your life. Later in this book, I will discuss another powerful method for overcoming problems and challenges.

The next way we can put our subconscious mind to work for us to help us in our lives is to give it an image to manifest, and the best way to do this, is to create a positive vision to dwell upon, often. The clearer the vision, and the more powerful the feelings you have towards its manifestation, the quicker it will appear. With that vision firmly implanted, the subconscious goes to work in conjunction with the Law of Attraction, more or less clarifying and magnetizing your thoughts, which allows the universe to respond to them.

The person who has a desired vision that is clear and positive for his life, starting at about three years into the future, is the person on the fast track to manifesting that vision and enjoying the success he desires.

As I mentioned in the first chapter, in my own life, one of the handful of absolutely critical factors, which contributed to the various successes I have enjoyed in multiple areas of my life, was creating a positive future vision. I mentioned already how I developed a vision of myself, six to seven years into the future, starting at age eleven, that I actively pursued. In the Bible Solomon says, "Where there is no vision, the people perish." (Proverbs 28:19) The opposite is also true. Where there is a vision, the person flourishes. Start by creating, in your own mind, a vision of your future success.

Here is another key area, where cultivating a positive vision is critical: the area of health and fitness. In this book, I will go into detail about the many strategies that I have learned from the martial arts and other various physical pursuits, on how to achieve and maintain optimal health and fitness

(See chapter eight). The starting point, of course, begins with *thinking* (thoughts become things). Developing a vision, and then reinforcing that vision by thinking similar thoughts and taking similar actions, is the key. Also, surrounding yourself with the right individuals, serves as a *vehicle* to drive you towards your goals. Fortunately for me, as a lifelong martial artist, I have often found myself surrounded by health- and fitness-minded individuals. Together, by controlling my thinking and associating with these types of people, I have found it much easier to develop the positive habits that would contribute to achieving my overall vision.

Long Term Thinking leads to Positive Habits

If I were to pinpoint the exact moment that had such a powerful influence on my commitment to health, it would be my sophomore year of college. I was enrolled in a public health class, and the instructor said something to me that caused an immediate shift in my thinking and my behavior, from that moment on. She said, "The habits you are developing, now, are the habits you will take with you, for the rest of your life."

My mind responded fully to that quote. I started thinking to myself, the eating habits I am developing now I will take with myself my entire life. The exercise habits, the money habits, the work habits--all of these habits will have an impact on my future. I started thinking fifteen years ahead, envisioning what my life might look like if I kept my current habits, and then I envisioned what it could look like if I committed to developing new and better habits. The vision that I developed for my mid-thirties became so exciting, that I started that very day working on my new habits. I would dwell on that vision often and, in doing so, would become more and more motivated to stick to my program of self-development, which was really starting to take off at that point in time. A good question to ask yourself when you find yourself repeating a habit, or when you are engaged in any regular behavior is, "What is this doing to me?" Better still, ask, "What will happen to me if I keep doing this without changing?"

Putting it All Together

In reviewing the fundamentals I have discussed thus far, we know that the starting point for everything we manifest in our life begins with our thoughts. Next the words we use have an extraordinary power as well. Improving the quality of our thoughts, and paying close attention to the words we speak, helps lay the foundation for creating the lives we truly desire. Applying long term positive thinking by developing a concrete vision of our future, guarantees that our lives travel in the direction of our choosing. You influence the journey, but you don't control everything you encounter along the way; that is the domain of the Universe. However, choosing the direction and deciding where you eventually intend on arriving, is up to you. If you don't choose a destination, other influences will choose it for you, and you may not like where you end up.

Actions lead quickest to results, and the first action you can take, which is perhaps the easiest, but also one of the more powerful, is to clearly write down your vision, as if it is happening now. Writing down your vision in the present, and in the positive, is very powerful for sending a clear message to your subconscious mind as to what you desire, and for magnetizing your thoughts with your desires.

Your vision should be concrete, but the methods you take to achieve your vision should be flexible. This is key. Let me repeat that again: your vision should be concrete, but the methods you take to achieve your vision should be flexible. Focus on the desire, but be detached on the approach. Begin now; take the first step, this instant, and write down a vision for your life, at least three years from now--ideally five to seven years into the future. Design your vision exactly the way you would like your life to be if the Universe lined up everything for you.

Typically, a vision can easily be broken down into a list of goals. Usually, the next step, after outlining your vision, is to list each goal separately and, then, go to work on accomplishing them. Later in this book, you will be introduced to a "goals workshop," which will help you to decide and design what you intend to manifest in your life. For now, begin to cultivate a vision for your life that will be nurtured, as you continue building your Warrior of Life program.

Your Success Vehicle

If you create a grand vision for yourself, oftentimes the goals are, also, very big. At least, this was the case for me, when I first created the vision for my own future. I realized that I needed a method to help me progress faster, and to overcome many of the obstacles that might get in the way. I realized that I needed a vehicle. The vehicle I chose, as I've already mentioned, was the martial arts. Since then, I have come to define what a vehicle must consist of, and, in doing so, I have realized that there are many ways to create an effective vehicle to achieve your vision. Creating a proper vehicle will put you on the fast track to achieving your goals, and it could save you many unnecessary years, in the process. Leveraging a vehicle is a core technique in the Warrior of Life program.

The primary component of the vehicle is the guide, someone who knows the way, who has been there before. A mentor or a coach is typically the guide. A mentor can show you the way, and a good coach can help you develop your skills and abilities, to stay on course. In addition to the guide, your vehicle needs other passengers. The passengers in a successful vehicle are like-minded individuals, who may have a different vision, but their destinations are in the same positive success-oriented direction. Napoleon Hill, in his many books on success, would refer to this group as your "mastermind alliance." The phrase, "Fly with the eagles," would also be talking about these types of people. In the chosen vehicle, you are the driver, and the purpose of that vehicle is to surround yourself with other achievers, while enlisting the guidance of a mentor and coach who can lead you towards your desired goal, or chosen area of success.

So once you've determined your vision, the next step is to create the vehicle to take you there. The starting point of creating the vehicle is to identify a coach and/or mentor. For example, if you are looking to improve your health and fitness, a good vehicle might be joining a class at the gym, joining Crossfit™, joining a master swimming club, hiring a personal trainer and nutritionist, or studying a yoga, to name a few. If you are looking to achieve financial independence, the next step might be to enlist the help of someone who is wealthy, for advice; to take a class in real estate or investing; to join an investors club, or to spend time with the CFO of your company.

A great way to achieve financial independence is through launching your own successful business. In this example, your business could be the potential vehicle; however, the vehicle is not complete until you find a coach and or mentor. An example of where you could find a great coach might be SCORE (Senior Corp of Retired Entrepreneurs). Next, you would want to create your mastermind. This might consist of sales and marketing experts, social media consultants, and a legal expert. Enlist the partnership of these individuals and you will have the components of a successful vehicle.

Chapter Summary

The starting point of manifesting your desires begins with controlling your thoughts and words. Next you create a vision, at least three years into the future, which is ideally how you want your life to appear. From the vision, you extract basic goals, to begin taking action upon. Finally, to fast track your progress, you create a vehicle, consisting of a coach and/or mentor, and an alliance of like-minded individuals to associate with, and who share similar ambitions.

Action Steps:

1. Develop a system for monitoring your thoughts and words. Perhaps, get a bracelet like the one described in this chapter to eliminate complaining from your speech.
2. Learn to pay attention to your feelings, especially when you are feeling bad. Use bad feelings as a trigger to change the thought you are currently thinking.
3. Take any problem or challenge you are currently facing and write it at the top of a blank piece of paper in the form of a question. Then, in a relaxed state of mind, write down as many solutions as possible. Aim for twenty. Take action on the best one.
4. Take a moment and write down a rough outline of your future vision. Schedule five to ten minutes throughout the day to mentally focus on this vision. The best times are ideally right before you go to sleep, and first thing, when you wake up.
5. Next, choose what may be a possible vehicle to help you arrive at your vision. Who is the guide? Who are along for the ride?

Chapter 3

Three Keys for the Journey

In the last chapter, we discovered the fundamentals for achieving the life we desire. In this chapter, I discuss several introductory mental techniques, which form a starting point for the Warrior of Life program. As you practice, these initial fundamental strategies the archetypical Warrior in you begins to develop, even though the journey you're embarked on is uniquely your own.

Act As If

When I was a child around the ages of six to ten, I used pretend that I was a character in a movie or comic book. Like most kids, I would dress up like fictional heroes such as Superman or Spiderman and run around the house and back yard with my brother acting out the part. Different from most kids that I knew, I wasn't satisfied, unless I had achieved the spitting image of the character I was portraying. My costume had to be complete; as in the case of Superman, I would wear red boots, blue pajamas, Superman Underoos, and a red cape, with my hair styled with the famous curl in the front. Then, I would do everything I could, to get myself into character.

With my mind's eye, I would visualize myself as Superman, while playing the part. One Saturday morning, when I was ten, I almost ended up at a Psychiatrist's office because, on this particular day, I thought I could make the play more exciting, by walking around on the roof dressed as Superman and by climbing in and out of the upstairs window. When my brother told my Mom that I was playing on the roof, she was a bit alarmed, to say the least. The truth is, I knew that I couldn't fly--the belief that I *was* Superman never crossed my mind; however, I was just looking for ways to make the character seem more real.

Fortunately, I never lost this quality of imagination. Fondly, I believe one of the many reasons I was attracted to the martial arts was because eventually as an adult I could still dress the part of the hero, donning martial arts uniforms or Ninja uniforms and practicing with Samurai weapons in class, while imagining I was in a historic battle. The fact is, combining props along with visualizing, in your mind's eye, the type of vision you want to manifest in your life, is a very powerful method for attracting the essence of your vision into your own life and for leveraging the "thoughts become things" universal law, to create your reality.

There is a common maxim in self-help literature which is to "act as if". This means, to act the part of the person you want to become, pretending to live the life you want to live. Many of the people I have coached, typically, have tried to make this approach work in their own life; however, they often go about it the wrong way. The mistake most of them make is, they act the part by trying to completely change the external. For instance, I've known people who have gone into financial debt, purchasing high priced items to help them "act as if" they are a wealthy individual. The problem with this approach is, they are focusing on the wrong side of the equation. Acting the part or "acting as if" works; however, the key to this approach is to change the inside. By inside, I mean your mind, attitudes, emotions, beliefs, and expectations. **If you change the inside, the outside will always take care of itself.** In this way, the props you use to help change the inside should not be putting you into debt. If your goal is to act the part of someone who is financially successful, what you are really trying to do is to feel as if you are financially successful now. You can't feel financially successful if you are going into debt.

40

"Act as if" is all about cultivating the feeling consistent with the desire.

Let me give an example of how I used this approach to overcome my fears and to become a proficient Skydiver. Typically, before each skydive I would get myself into a resourceful state of mind, the same way you might see professional athletes doing it before a big game. I would essentially psych myself up with positive self-talk, breathing exercises, and physical gestures of power like squeezing my fists. This would provide a temporary change in my behavior but no lasting change; however, the method that worked the best for me was the same game I played when I was six: I would pretend. After ten training jumps with my instructor, in which I used the aforementioned approach to controlling my behavior, I was ready for my first solo skydive. There, on my first solo skydive, sitting in the back of the plane, I got the idea to "act as if" I was the fictional spy, James Bond. I started putting a lot of energy into this particular visualization. While seeing myself in my mind's eye as James Bond, I also started to adapt the physical mannerisms I expected of him, which I knew from watching how the character was portrayed in movies. I narrowed my gaze, lowered my breathing and started to feel this cool confidence well up inside of me, as I worked to demonstrate it in my physical persona. As a result, when I got to the door of the plane, almost three miles above the ground, instead of feeling fear, I was instead in character, feeling a sense of confidence and purpose. I even imagined that the people who had just left the plane were the "bad guys," and I was chasing after them. Without a moment's hesitation, I leaped from the plane and enjoyed an exciting jump back to the drop zone. I repeated this approach a bunch of times, really enjoying the game I was playing. Eventually, I got to the point where I didn't need to act as if anymore. I developed the qualities and confidence I sought. They became a part of me. That is how the technique to "act as if" is supposed to work. You go to work on transforming the inside, and the outside takes care of itself.

There is an advanced version of this technique that is a core component of the Warrior of Life program. Instead of trying to identify someone out there to act the part of, another powerful approach is to create a vision of yourself with the qualities and characteristics you desire, and then to act out that part. The key to making this work is to invest the necessary amount of time into visualization. For instance, the reason I was able to act the part of James Bond is because I had seen many James Bond movies on the TV and movie theater screen. To use this approach, you have to visualize yourself on the screen of your mind enough times in advance, performing in the manner you desire, so that it is easy for you to replicate in real-time. To make this work you need to be focusing on the qualities you want to possess, by identifying them in your environment. In your natural environment, you may see these qualities demonstrated by a mentor or coach, at a seminar, in a book, or even in a movie. Once you've identified the quality, the next step is to see yourself with your mind's eye possessing the quality. Finally, you perform as if you've had those qualities all along.

When I was starting out in sales, I would watch how the successful salespeople performed. Then, I would imagine myself performing in the same way. In my imagination, I would have the confidence and the persuasive skills I longed for. As a result, shortly thereafter, I could go into an important sales meeting being fully myself, but with the confidence and skills I had mastered by observing others and rehearsing it in my own mind.

On the other hand, when I am studying a new martial art, if it is available I would read a book or watch a video of a master of that martial art. Then, I would go to class acting as if I was that individual, endeavoring to move as he moves and to perform as he performs. In every case, I eventually started to manifest the skills and characteristics of that person as a natural part of my own skill.

For instance, growing up, I became a huge admirer of an amazing martial artist out of Nebraska named Robert Bussey. Bussey had travelled to Japan to study the martial art of ninjutsu and then came back and developed his own system combining ninjutsu with other martial arts he had studied, along with his resolute philosophy that every technique must be practical and effective in real combat. Bussey was and still is a very prolific author and wrote many articles for martial arts magazines. He also authored a book about ninjutsu, and he was profiled in a book by his student. In addition, he created two series of video instruction in his system. Well, I read everything of his I could get my hands on, and I practiced his movements in front of the TV, eventually learning everything he demonstrated on all of his videos, performing it much like he was doing on the screen. In addition, whenever I went to class I would "act as if" I was him as I performed self-defense techniques on my training partners. A few years later, I had the opportunity to finally train with him in person and, judging by the way he interacted with me, I imagine it must have been uncanny how much of his technique and movement he saw expressed by me.

Building on the previous lesson, once you have a vision of your desires, manifesting those desires begins on the inside and works itself outwards. The quickest way to build the inside consistent with your desires is to act the part of a person who has manifested those things in their own lives. This is how I changed myself, at age thirteen, when I began the martial arts. I would act the part of the people I admired, absorbing their various characteristics, and I would combine this with the practice of imagining myself, performing in a manner consistent with the vision I held for my life.

Identify ways to begin applying "act as if" now. How would you behave if you had already manifested your vision and major life goals? If you are faced with a challenge, who is someone you can think of, either fictional or real, who could easily surmount the challenge? Channel their skills and behaviors by acting the part in your own life. Anything that you could want to manifest has most likely been demonstrated, in some form, by someone else. This means that your ability to model their behavior and achieve the same thing is virtually unlimited. For example, if your area is business, identify the leaders in your industry. Next, learn all you can about them from books, videos, and, if possible, personal interaction. Finally, "act as if" you have been performing like them, all along. Whether it is through confident sales presentations, smooth negotiations, or public speaking to large audiences, use these individuals as models to guide your own behavior. Before long, people will be emulating you, too!

Introspection and Self-Analysis

Warrior of Life is an inner program of the mind. As warriors, the only thing we need to do battle with are the negative thoughts that have invaded our minds and that show up in some form of limiting factor in our lives. Our doubts, fears, worries, and limiting beliefs are examples of these limitations. Once we eradicate them from our minds and replace them with thoughts of

43

confidence and power, as well as beliefs that serve us, then our success becomes practically guaranteed.

I wrote in the first chapter about how, when I was a teenager, I wandered into the self-help section at the bookstore, and my life forever changed. The truth is, I wasn't looking for help. Help means that your assistance comes from something outside of you. I didn't want help; I was seeking self-transformation. Self-transformation is something that happens *inside* of you and shows up on the *outside* in your attitude, your behavior, your actions, and your results. Self-transformation says, "I can improve." That is the aim of this book, to help individuals to become better, by improving the inside first.

For most of my life I have been committed to personal growth and self-transformation. To reach this aim, I have read over a thousand books, five hundred of which have earned a spot in my personal library to be read and re-read again. I have listened to over a hundred different audio programs repeatedly in my car, and I have attended seminars and workshops led by the best in their respective fields. In addition, I have interviewed countless successful individuals from all walks of life, and a fundamental behavior I have identified among all high achievers is their willingness to self-analyze. Analyzing their behaviors and reflecting on their results to determine what things are working for them and which aren't, is something these top people do on a regular basis. I personally consider my willingness to consistently examine myself open-mindedly, and then make improvements as often as needed, to be the driving force behind my growth and achievement.

In order for someone to fully benefit from this practice, they must, at once, fully accept responsibility for everything that has happened in their life. To analyze yourself, and then to take actions to improve, you cannot give control to anything outside of yourself. You must accept that everything which happens in your life happens because of you. For many this is a tough pill to swallow. In fact, most people I teach this principle to fight me tooth and nail on this. In my own life, this was difficult for me to accept as well. However, the moment I accepted that everything in my life was because of me--that the stuff I deemed bad was my fault, and the good was, fortunately, my fault too--my positive self-transformation accelerated. To this day, this belief continues to support me, by giving me the ability to analyze everything that happens to me, in way that gives me full control to change myself and affect future outcomes. By resolutely accepting full responsibility for every aspect of your life, the Warrior way of thinking takes hold in your mind and the "victim mentality" that many cling to begins to weaken, eventually, being destroyed.

Let me give you an example of this, in action, as it relates to business. A few years ago, I was negotiating with the owner of a fitness center, to conduct one of my popular health and fitness workshops for her client base. She was very open to it, and she offered a sixty/forty percent split of all the revenue with the sixty going to her for owning the space/clients and the forty going to me. Looking back I realize that this split would have been very favorable for me. We would have both made a profit, and I would have a new client base for future events and products. However, at that moment I wasn't focused on the benefits. I had just finished listening to a series of audio cd's on negotiation, and I saw this as an opportunity to apply what I had learned. Well at the end of the negotiation, she agreed to an eighty/twenty percent split with me getting the eighty. Victory was mine, or so it seemed for a moment. Guess how many of her clients she encouraged to come to this event? Guess how committed she was to seeing it succeed? If you answered "not any" and "not at all" you are correct. So following this experience, I took the time to analyze the situation taking full responsibility for everything. I came to realize that I could have said yes to the sixty/forty and we both could have benefited immensely. I would also bet that she would have accepted fifty-fifty and still put in all of her effort to make the workshop a success. I decided to learn from this and to change my approach going forward. Now my business partners know me for being extremely generous with profit sharing, and more and more people are signing up to work with me. This realization never could have happened if I took the easy road and labeled her as a "jerk" and didn't take the time to analyze myself in relation to the situation. By the way, this is just one of many other similar examples that have taken place in my life. The important thing is to learn from them. I have known many people who have never taken the time to analyze any situation in the same way as the one just presented, from the viewpoint of full responsibility. As a result, these people will go for twenty or thirty years encountering the same problems in different forms, always getting the same lousy results. If they applied what I am presenting here, they could in that instant make a change that would have a dramatic positive impact on the results they attract and enjoy for the rest of their lives.

The key is to begin taking responsibility for everything in your life, and to analyze yourself in relation to what's going good in your life and what is not going so good. Then, implement personal changes. If your boss doesn't pay you enough, analyze what you can do to be deserving of more pay. Instead of blaming the boss and company policies, put the responsibility squarely on yourself. Bring more value, and you will get more pay, if not there, definitely somewhere else. The problem is that most people live with the philosophy of "if they pay me more, then I will work harder." Life doesn't work that way. It is like telling the fireplace, warm up the house, and then I will put in some wood.

If someone doesn't keep a commitment to you, analyze what you can do to be more clear in your communication in future arrangements. Don't just label the person as irresponsible, even if they seem to be. Use it as a chance to improve yourself. Become so clear in scheduling appointments with others for example, that they will do anything not to be late for a meeting with you. The masters of life use everything as a learning experience and an opportunity to grow.

Unfortunately, too many people go through their life as a "victim". The victim never accepts responsibility for anything in his life unless it's something that has gone well and he can take the credit. The victim speaks of excuses and blame. Victims typically don't analyze their own behavior and personal communication. Instead, they become fixated on how everyone else should behave. This is why victims never really succeed. They think they know how everyone else can change; however, they obviously have no control over the other person. Instead, if the victim gave up on that role and accepted full responsibility for his own life, then he could analyze ways he could change himself. Since our behavior is something we have control over, then the option to change now has the possibility of actually taking place. You can't change other people, so why give them any power or control over you? Realize that, every time you blame, you are giving someone else power over you. Powerlessness leads to despair. A Warrior of Life accepts full responsibility for everything in his life and in doing this he instantly has all the power. To the Warrior of Life, all things are an opportunity for improvement and growth, especially his challenges and difficulties.

As I wrote earlier, I am still amazed that I had the wisdom to accept responsibility for the fact that I was a target of bullies. Whereas most people would blame the bullies, I chose to analyze what it was about me that made me a target. In doing the self-analysis, I discovered quite a few characteristics of my personality, beliefs, and behavior that I didn't desire to have anymore. This became the starting point for all the positive transformation that unfolded next in my life. It's horrifying when we read stories about children in the newspaper who are bullied. Even more horrifying is when they respond to bullying by blaming the bully and resorting to violence in the form of bringing weapons to school to harm others and themselves. When I've presented this perspective on accepting responsibility at my speaking events, I've had participants come up to me later to ask me if I am saying it's the person being bullied who is to blame. I respond to this by saying, "I recognize that some bullies are just bad eggs; however, if the person being bullied doesn't accept total responsibility, how can he have any chance to improve the situation and his life?"

The doorway to achievement and success begins to open when we view everything as a gift towards our growth and development. The universe is just a mirror of ourselves, and the people and circumstances in our lives are reflecting back to us both the things we deem good and the things we deem bad. Recognize the things showing up in your life that you like, and do more of what's attracting them. Also, identify the things which you don't like, and develop a strategy to change what it is about you that's attracting them. This includes how you allow people to treat you. Realize, you determine ultimately how people treat you, by how you behave. By choosing personal responsibility over blame, you can alter your behavior and thereby affect how you are received by the world.

The fastest way to begin using the tool of self-analysis and introspection in your life is to ask yourself various questions "why?" Why am I doing this? Why do I do it this way? Why does this bother me? Why do things like this keep happening to me? *A great trigger to get yourself to ask "why" about something, is when you have a bad feeling.* If something doesn't feel good, take the time to examine why? Then replace the cause of the bad feeling with a new behavior, and the effect will take care of itself.

Remember that all cause is internal. If you want to change your effects, you must change the cause, and that begins with your thinking.

At this point in the book, I'd like to recommend you purchase a journal. As a Warrior of Life, the journal is a necessary piece of equipment. This journal will at first be a book of empty pages, and it is your responsibility to fill these pages with items of value that you can come back to again and again, at different times, to refer to on your path of personal development and success. This is not a diary of your daily activities. Instead, a journal is a convenient place to record your ideas, as well as all the good ideas you may come across. In addition, it is the place to record your goals and your progress, as well as to analyze, on paper, the various challenges you may encounter and how you intend to deal with those challenges. I have been keeping a journal since I was in college. Currently, I have fifteen journals, all dated, each with a collection of motivational tidbits, success strategies, ideas, goals, sermons, lessons, lectures, personal anecdotes, personal challenges and solutions. I have all this and a whole host of other valuable nuggets of wisdom, which I can continue to go back to and digest again and again.

A core maxim of the Warrior of Life that guides his behavior is, "Do the things that others won't do." Create a life that others can emulate by being an example of what's possible. Begin with a journal. Carry it with you. Make it part of your key possessions along the Warrior path.

Personal Success Rules

As I mentioned earlier, at the age of thirteen, when my parents enrolled me in martial arts lessons, I wasn't just going there to learn this new discipline; I was going there to change my life. I had already determined that this would be the vehicle I would use to change my habits of thinking, my attitude, my behaviors and actions, and, ultimately, my results. Since no one else knew what my ultimate reason for studying the martial arts was--not my parents--not the instructor--I realized that, if this was going to work, I was going to have to augment the martial arts training with other strategies. This is how I stumbled on the practice of setting "personal success rules". The week before my very first lessons began, I started to develop a list, in my mind, of behaviors I was going to give up, and of new behaviors I was going to put in place. I also started to create a list of higher standards for myself that I committed myself to keeping. Because my commitment was so big, and my discipline in keeping the rules I established for myself was so strict, I was able to achieve the results I desired. In addition, I continue to practice the martial arts to this day, while continually striving to constantly improve myself (pay attention to other core characteristics of the Warrior of Life and how often they show up in this book, such as the qualities of discipline, persistence, and raising standards).

The rules I established at that time were personal, and are still personal, to me. If you were to read them all you might think them silly; however, within in the context of my life at that particular time, they fit naturally. I mentioned a few in chapter one. Let me share some of those along with an analysis of why I chose each one:

1. "Only cry in sorrow never in pain." I wanted to be tough. I was a whiny kid. I no longer desired to be this way. I thought of this rule every time I got hurt and kept it. I became so adept at practicing this rule, that a year later I dislocated my finger and fractured my hand while playing football, and, because I didn't whine or cry, my parents thought it was just a bruise. My overprotective and very caring mom waited an entire week before she decided to take me to the doctor, and that was only because, a week later, my finger was stuck in place, and I couldn't get it to move. She was in shock when the doctor diagnosed the injury.

2. The previous rule evolved into "not whining about anything." Currently, I practice the "no complaining" rule. I monitor my speech to make sure I don't complain. This and the previous rule have had a definite effect on my ability to process the various events that happen in life. These rules have definitely changed my inside quality of mind. They've made it better, made me more powerful. For example, in 2006, in a fluke accident while running through the Humphrey Terminal in Minnesota's airport at five in the morning, carrying my suitcase over my shoulder, I tore my Achilles tendon while trying to leap up the stairs. I should have stretched first, but didn't have time (hence, the reason I was running). Anyway, I made the flight home to New York with a completely ruptured

tendon and then went to the emergency room in my hometown located in Connecticut. I was there for several more hours because the attending physician was having trouble diagnosing my injury, since she had been told the pain associated with a tendon rupture is equivalent to a gunshot wound. I wasn't registering any such pain. It dawned on me later that day that my pain monitor might not be the same as other people's anymore. In other words, I apparently experience intense pain the same way someone might a minor ache. I believe this to be the power of the mind-body connection in action. Study this in your own life, especially during your own times of self-analysis.

3. My next rule of which I frequently reminded myself especially during martial arts training was, "Whenever you fall down, always jump to your feet." This rule came to me one day watching the advanced martial arts class train. I saw a black belt get taken down unexpectedly and within a nanosecond he was back on his feet taking down his opponent. I decided in that instant that I would perform that way, and I went ahead to make it a rule. To reinforce this rule, I would play the "video" of this person jumping to his feet, over and over again, in my mind. Later, I realized that this rule had become a metaphor for my life. Now, whenever I experience a setback, I go into a state of mind that drives me to respond by immediately bouncing back in the direction of my choosing.

Another very cool aspect of the martial arts, which I often like to mention, are the skills of rolling and break-falling I learned. People often ask me if I ever had to use my martial arts training. I know they mean, "Have I had to physically defend myself?" However, whenever I am asked this, the fact comes to mind that I have used rolling and break-falling numerous times in my life to prevent serious injury. On several occasions while skydiving, if it hadn't been for my ability to roll, I could have experienced a serious injury. This is a metaphor for life as well. Learning to roll, to go with the force instead of against it, is a very practical way to let challenges and obstacles dissipate on their own. This is why I believe, if you study the martial arts deeply, you find countless metaphors for life. A goal of this book is to share those teachings to the non-martial artist in a way that is practical and effective. So practice this rule in your own life; whenever you fall (or experience a setback), jump to your feet (make a comeback).

4. "Train all the time." This rule, and various permutations of it, have changed my life. Whereas, in the martial arts, many of my classmates would practice only during a regular class, I would practice some aspect of the martial arts every chance I got. I was always practicing something. When working around the house, I was practicing physical movements. When enjoying a nice day at the beach, I would work drills on the sand and in the surf. When walking to and from my car I always practice awareness. As a result, this practice evolved into cultivating a natural awareness of my surroundings I consider to be consistent with that of the historic Samurai (referred to in Japanese as Zanshin).

Also, I apply this rule with my fitness as well. Currently, I am known to drop down and do push-ups while at the office, while waiting for a train at the station, while watching TV, etc. There is no rule, at least not for me, that the only place to train is the gym. Instead, my rule is, "Train all the time." You can change the word "train" to practice, exercise, read, study, list ideas, or network. It's a life changing rule that I highly recommend. For example, a large portion of my career has been in various sales roles. In these roles, I have enjoyed tremendous success. The reason is, I continually applied this rule by reading sales books, attending seminars, and role-playing sales situations, even when outside of work.

The more you engage in a discipline, the more the discipline engages you, causing you to expand in ways not yet even imaginable. So do the things you need to do to succeed as often as possible by putting in the training time.

Personal Success Rules are not just something to keep stored in your mind, you can also write them in your journal, and refer back to them often to reflect on your progress. Determining all of your own rules is a powerful practice for shaping your mind and strengthening your character. In the chapter on health and fitness you will learn of some of my other rules as they pertain to practicing health.

Act as If, Introspection, and Personal Success Rules are just a handful of the mental techniques I discovered and utilized early on in my own life. I believe these made it possible for me to progress more rapidly, as well as make immediate use of the additional mental techniques I came to learn. Throughout this book, you will learn many more techniques and strategies, like these, that you can begin using immediately. The reason I chose these for this chapter is because they encompass a variety of other success principles built into their practice. Plus, they form the basis for experiencing immediate changes in your life.

Chapter Summary

The key to changing or improving anything begins with the first step, and that first step is, always, taking control of your thoughts. Don't just read this book passively, instead, take the ideas presented, and apply them immediately in your own life. You can begin "acting as if" this very moment. You can also put this book aside, grab your journal and begin *reflecting* on the type of vision you intend to manifest, the possible solutions to challenges you are facing, or even answers to life's questions you are pondering. You can also decide this very instant what you will no longer tolerate in your life. You can decide what behavior you will give up and what behavior you will reinforce. You can set the rules that help you to win the game of life, and you can do all of that right now before reading another sentence. Many who read this won't do it; those of you who go on to succeed will. Let this be you!

Action Steps:

1. Get a journal. Commit to writing in it, beginning today, and for the rest of your life.
2. In your journal, answer the questions: What is going well in my life? What would I like to change?
3. Choose something you desire. Determine who has it already. Identify what character traits and behaviors that person possesses that allowed him or her to manifest the thing you desire. Model them by "acting as if" you possess those same traits and behaviors.
4. Schedule time, each day, to reflect. One suggestion is, examine what rules you may have set for yourself. Determine if these are working.
5. Set new rules for yourself to guide your behavior towards the achievement of your goals.
6. Keep your journal nearby and continue to record ideas, strategies, and plans for your life's success.

Chapter 4

Connecting with Spirit

One of the great things about the martial arts, in general, is that they present a holistic practice, meaning that they combine the mental and physical components with the spiritual, to create a complete system of human development. The Warrior of Life program is based on this approach and endeavors to help you strengthen and improve your mind, your body, and your Spiritual connection, thereby creating a total human being.

Although the first martial art I studied didn't focus as much on the Spiritual, I could feel myself being pulled in that direction, even while still a teenager. When I began to read books that discussed spirituality as it pertained to the martial arts, I was drawn to delve further, by studying eastern religions and esoteric sciences, such as Taoist Yoga, and others. Then, as I already mentioned, certain events occurred which inspired me to make spiritual growth a priority in my life. As I started to become more and more interested in this type of study, through the law of attraction and my reticular cortex, doors appeared for me to walk through to further expand my growth...

Martial Arts present an excellent metaphor for life. For example, the ranking system provides a proven framework for setting and achieving goals. In this example, the black belt typically represents the major end goal, though, when you finally achieve it, you realize it's just the beginning. Then, on the way to black belt are smaller short-term goals corresponding to a different color belt. As the student progress up the belt ranks, he develops greater skills and abilities that build on the previous lessons. Intrinsic in this approach is the realization that the road to black belt is a journey, and the key to achievement is to keep one eye on the major goal, while intently focusing on each part of the journey.

Just like in life, there is a phenomenon in the martial arts, where the majority of students who commit to the journey will typically quit before they achieve their major goal, many quitting at the belt right before black belt. As someone goes through this process and eventually achieves their goal of black belt, they have by that point ideally developed the quality of persistence. With this quality they can now transfer their ability to persist to any goal they set for themselves, thereby becoming someone who truly achieves whatever they set their mind to.

"Stay the path" is the common maxim that you often here being spouted by the senior ranks. This maxim always resonated with me, as it is very similar to "long term thinking" and, contained within it, is the active quality of persistence. Long term thinking which I have mentioned earlier was something that I had developed naturally and then reinforced once I starting reading about it in motivation tomes.

The reality of life is that, once you achieve the goal you set for yourself and arrive at that new "vista," you typically find that the top of the mountain was just the bottom of another, even bigger mountain, and the climb begins again. When I earned my black belt, I looked out on the horizon, and I realized, there was so much more to learn and so much more to develop within myself. One area in particular I was drawn to was the area of spirituality. At first, it was just an interest that I gave some attention to; then, after a serious head on automobile collision, after which I took the time to reflect on my own mortality, my interest in Spirituality and discovering a connection to something much larger than myself became a compelling goal. Thanks to the Law of Attraction and my reticular cortex, the more I focused on it, the more opportunities I found to broaden my study.

Spiritual Training

The first opportunity I took advantage of was a Dzogchen Buddhist Center which was located a few blocks from where I was attending college. Dzogchen Buddhism is a form of Tibetan Buddhism. Every Sunday, I would go there for most of the morning. From eight until ten in the morning, the head lama (teacher) would teach a practical life lesson based on Buddhist doctrine. Then, from ten to eleven-thirty, we would all meditate. From eleven-thirty to twelve, we would help prepare lunch, after which we would share a vegetarian meal together. I did this every Sunday for two years while I was in school. During the week in between each Sunday's service at the center, I would sit in my bedroom each night and meditate for a half hour or so. (The cushions I got to meditate on were handmade from a place in Vermont called Samadhi Cushions. I still have them and have meditated on them for over fifteen years, and I believe they are still successfully in business.) The practice of meditation, which I first developed at the Dzogchen Center, is something that I continue to do to this day and that I will discuss in more detail in this book. Meditation is a key component in the Warrior of Life program, and it is the gateway to many benefits, such as improved health; access to greater faculties of the mind, such as intuition, and creative thinking; as well the most direct method for experiencing first hand that connection to something bigger than ourselves, which I wrote about earlier.

During this time in my life, I started studying other martial arts, especially those that had a spiritual component. One was Budo Taijutsu at a school in Wallingford, CT, whose curriculum also encompassed traditional Togakure Ryu Ninjutsu. This particular martial art had the most diverse curriculum of any I had studied, and it included mental training, physical techniques, weapons, and a spiritual practice designed to awaken spiritual abilities in the individual, such as intuition. This art had a formula (typically called the "way") to combine a variety of different self-defense skills into a natural, flowing motion that was practical and effective. This system appealed to me, and I continue to study it, on and off looking for ways to combine its principles with the variety of other disciplines I was, and continue to be, engaged in.

Once I finished college and started working full-time, I had much more money to invest in my training, and hired a Chi-Gung master to teach me Chi-Gung on a personal student basis. Chi-Gung is a Chinese martial art and healing system that cultivates the body's natural spiritual energy to improve healing, mental ability, and physical martial arts. The bulk of Chi-Gung practice revolves around meditation. Different from traditional meditation practice, which is typically done sitting, Chi-Gung is practiced as both a sitting and a standing meditation, as well as, as a moving meditation that incorporates deep breathing, visualization, and fluid body movements. Tai-Chi is a popular martial art with its roots in Chi-Gung.

At this same time, I also began studying Reiki. I had read in the newspaper about a woman who had a Reiki practice in New Haven, CT, and whose lineage was a direct line from the founder of the Usui Reiki system. I immediately sought her out to begin studying Reiki. (Reiki is a Spiritual system originating in Japan that seems similar to Chi-Gung in its use of energy, except with Reiki, the energy comes from outside the body and is transmitted to another person with the intent to heal, by using one's own body as the conduit. In harnessing this energy, both participants enjoy the benefits.) I studied this system for several years, eventually becoming a Reiki Master in the lineage.

I mention these experiences, not only to demonstrate the breadth of my devotion to developing the spiritual in my life, but also to show how cultivating a strong vision allows the Law of Attraction to provide many opportunities in which to choose a vehicle to manifest that vision. Also during this time, I had the pleasure of studying with several Spiritual guides while developing friendships, some to this day, with other like-minded seekers. It seemed, the more I immersed myself in thinking and focusing on expanding my spiritual practice, the more opportunities appeared. Eventually, this led me to a very exciting introduction to a real Native American medicine man I'll call Roaring Brook, who I fondly referred to as the "witch doctor" because of his work as a healer. I soon came to learn that Roaring Brook's people had been "connecting directly with spirit" for generations, and he was willing to share his knowledge outside of his race.

Like many ancient traditions, Roaring Brook's people had developed practices (such as chanting, dance, sweat lodges, vision quests) all designed to raise one's energy and open their awareness to realms beyond the physical, in the aim of achieving a direct connection and communication with what they call Spirit (which is another word for Source, Creator, God, Energy, or Higher Power). I saw this relationship with Roaring Brook as a wonderful opportunity to fast track my own spiritual growth by immersing myself in his practices.

Studying with a Witch Doctor

In the fall of 2001, I was invited to Roaring Brook's home in Hunt Valley, Maryland for the weekend to take part in several traditional ceremonies, including a sweat lodge. This would be the first of several times that I was to be involved in ceremonies with Roaring Brook, and one of many times that I would travel far from home to study with a notable teacher. A funny anecdote came out of the first meeting: the person who introduced me told me to bring a certain type of flower (which I forget now what type) and to bring tobacco as a gift. Being a non-smoker I had never purchased any tobacco product and did not know the first thing about it. So I went to the tobacco shop in town and grabbed a bag of tobacco off the counter. In a rush, I made the purchase and headed out without really ever looking at the pouch. I took the train to Baltimore, caught the Metro to the last stop on a particular line, telephoned Roaring Brook's apprentice on the phone, and someone was sent to pick me up and bring me to his place. That night, I met everyone who was attending for the weekend and retired to bed. The next morning, Roaring Brook and I met in a private room, where he did healings and counseling, and I offered the two gifts. He smiled and then beckoned for the people outside the room, mostly comprised of his followers/students, to come in to see what I had given him. In my naiveté, without even realizing it, I had given him a package of "Red Man Chewing Tobacco". He thought it was funny, especially since I didn't initially realize the faux pas: buying chewing tobacco and, worse, buying a brand called Red Man and giving it to Native American. He clearly had a great sense of humor, and as I was around him more, it became clear that he was a truly enlightened person who could see things the rest of us typically can't. For example, during one of his "healing sessions," where he was counseling a person who was suffering from on-going painful headaches, nausea, lack of energy, and depression, he sat directly in front of her, separated by a piece of leather, with diagrams on it drawn in chalk. He gave her a handful of stones and told her to drop them on the leather. (I am not sure what the arrangement of the stones translated to mean to him, although I am certain they meant something.) At that point he began asking her questions about her life, many extremely personal, relating to decisions she had made many years before. I could see her becoming visibly upset, eventually becoming sick. Then her posture began to change, color returned to her face, she wiped away the tears that had begun accumulating around her eyes. She thanked him and left. I asked him later what had happened and he told me that she was being tormented by demons, and he helped her release them from her life. I thought he was speaking metaphorically until he said, "you wouldn't believe the things I see during the sweat lodge." This "seeing" ability piqued my interest further and fueled my quest for greater esoteric spiritual knowledge and ability.

During our lessons together, Roaring Brook talked to me about what I had already come to know as chakras. The word chakra originates in Hindu texts and refers to energy centers located in various parts of the human body. Though he had a different term for them, I was amazed to discover that both Native Americans and eastern monks had discovered the same subtle spiritual energies and energy vortexes, and both had mapped out their correlation to the human body. Just like with Chi-Gung and Reiki, I came to realize, these ceremonies I participated in were another method to refine and direct the energy circulating through the human body.

Warrior traditions like those practiced by Native American tribes, Shaolin Kung-Fu masters, and the Samurai are steeped in spirituality. Just like those traditions, the Warrior of Life program is as much a spiritual growth program as it is a success system. As you practice the mental success strategies throughout this book and begin to achieve your goals, I don't want you to arrive there, saying to yourself, "Is this all there is?" Expanding your spiritual connection to your Source (Creator) fills that void while connecting you to a stream of well-being which helps you to flow towards your goals more rapidly and with ease, instead of struggling for a lifetime.

Fundamental Spiritual Principles

I was raised a Catholic, and, when I became an adult and began defining what I desired from my spiritual path, I moved beyond the study of Catholicism to studying multiple religions and systems. As you just have read, this included experiences learning Buddhism and studies with a Native American Witch Doctor, just to name a few, as well as a deep search into the spiritual side of the martial arts. In doing so, I experienced some very deep esoteric teachings, some of which I will be sharing in this book; however, it dawned on me, one day, that perhaps the greatest spiritual teacher to ever walk the planet, Jesus the Christ, didn't tell his followers to sit cross-legged, with the heel of the left foot in line with their perineum, with the tip of their tongue against the roof of their mouth, their head tilted down, and their eyes closed, with their eyeballs gazing at the point between their eyebrows, while visualizing with each breath the joining of primordial energy stored at the base of the spine being linked with the brain by traveling upward through the chakras in a continuous orbit (another esoteric practice I learned). Or perhaps he did share this with a certain few of his disciples who had mastered the fundamentals on the Spiritual path. The fundamentals are those teachings which we read about in the New Testament of the Bible, which serve as the basics of following his example, and include the following: to practice gratitude in all things, to forgive, to go the extra mile, to think positively, to have faith, to love thy neighbor, and to detach from possessions and circumstances (to name just a few).

Five hundred years earlier, another Spiritual teacher, Siddhartha Gautama--commonly referred to as the Buddha--was teaching his followers more or less the same fundamental principles. He commonly taught that the gateway to the spiritual realms, and ultimately enlightenment, was through the mind, the mental faculty of man. In this chapter, we will build a spiritual practice that will organically unfold as we begin, by refining the nature of our thoughts to match the totality of our being.

Gratitude

Gratitude is one of the highest vibration thoughts that we can reach. It is always associated with positive feelings and emotions. Many sages consider thoughts of gratitude to be the closest form of energy to Source energy. To walk in a state of perpetual gratitude is to walk with the masters. For the Warrior of Life, the starting point of spiritual development is to begin with gratitude. There are many reasons to practice gratitude in your life which I will discuss in a moment. From a spiritual perspective, one of our main purposes of doing this every day, and throughout the day, is to raise our energy.

At first, this appears as if it would be easy, just to be thankful and grateful for the many good things and blessings in our life; however, once we've taken the time to express gratitude for our blessings, then we must take the time to express gratitude for the things we wouldn't typically give thanks for, such as our challenges, our problems, the people in our lives who we perceive have wronged us, and current, as well as past, difficult experiences. This is where the challenge begins, and this is why the warrior's path is not for everyone. Most people won't put in the mental effort necessary to rise above the negativity and express gratitude, for anything and everything (and I mean everything) in their life.

The starting point for the Warrior of Life is to cultivate gratitude, for anything and everything in our lives. This is the gateway. This is the skill of the master. You can't increase your vibration and purify your Spirit if you harbor negativity in various forms. You must release those negative vibrations, and the mechanism is through the purifying power of gratitude. The more you can be thankful for the challenges in your life, the more you weaken the "victim" mindset, allowing your true power to emerge. From this position of power, you can change the things you no longer desire to experience. One of the keys is to be grateful for what you have, on the way to what you want.

In order to be grateful for everything in your life, you must give up the victim role. As you've already learned, a Warrior of Life refuses to ever be a victim for anything. This means taking responsibility for everything that happens to us and, then, (and this is the best part) choosing what things and events are going to mean for us. For example, in the Autumn of 2006, I was on the tail end of a whirlwind business trip, which began in Chicago, took me to Miami, had a brief stint in New York (close to where I live, but no time to stop home) and then took me to Minneapolis. As I've already mentioned, on my final day away, I was running to catch a 6 AM flight. My body was cold and stiff, and I was carrying, over my shoulder, my suitcase, which weighed fifty pounds, and I attempted to sprint up a flight of stairs. Well, my knee went past my foot, and, on the ascent, I ruptured my Achilles tendon. In the hospital, eventually (I already talked about how it took a while to diagnose me), I learned that I needed surgery and that my recovery would take no less than six months. Upon learning that, the victim thoughts started to flood my mind, but, being a student of these teachings, I immediately took conscious control of my mind, and I gave it a new thought to dwell upon. This was, "What are the benefits of this injury?"

Knowing that the mind can only concentrate on one thought at a time, I gave it a positive thought upon which to focus. Eventually, I came up with nine different things that the injury could mean, and, then, I turned them into goals with actions. As a result of this injury, I completely revolutionized my nutrition and exercise program; I ran my first marathon; I got into the best shape of my life, and I developed a deeper connection to my spiritual source through long periods of meditation, which the immobility because of my injury allowed. Back then and still, today, I am truly grateful for all the benefits this injury provided, and, of course, for the injury itself. In fact, whenever I look back on this injury, I discover even more benefits, such as the experience of my parents and my wife going out of their way to care for me and the appreciation I hold for their care. There are more examples: my brother showering me with gifts of movies and TV shows on DVD to help me pass the time I'd be laid up, my colleagues helping me to move around the office, and much, much more. The more I saw these things, the more I came to realize how truly blessed I am, and, the truth is, you are as truly blessed.

Here are some key points to remember when cultivating gratitude in your life. First, the mind can only concentrate on one thought at a time, so make it a good one. Second, begin each day orienting your mind in the right direction by listing audibly, or on paper, at least five things you are grateful for. As you say or write each one, take a moment to see the thing in your mind, and fully feel the feelings of gratitude for it.

Third, when you are presented with a challenge or a difficult situation, ask yourself, "What about this can I be thankful for?" If you have a pressing problem that you need to find a solution for, you actually make it easier for your mind to find a positive solution, if you take your mind off the negativity associated with the problem by focusing on positive feelings of gratitude.

Forgiveness

On the opposite side of the same coin, is forgiveness. Whereas gratitude works to raise your vibration and purify (make positive) your energy, forgiveness releases blocks that may be hampering the flow of energy through your body. The ancient Chinese Masters recognized that everything is energy, and that our bodies are, also, energy. They mapped out the flow of energy through the body via what they called meridians (which act like power lines of the body) and chakras. The chakras are described as spinning energy vortexes. Chinese medicine teaches that our health--the health of our bodies--is affected by the operation of these spinning vortexes, of which there are seven main ones. They also stated that energy blocks, caused by harboring painful emotions, are one of the primary reasons why the meridians would become blocked, or why the chakras' spinning would slow. When either of these things happens, illness and aging sets in. The key to perfect health is to release these emotions, allowing the energy to flow naturally again, thus restoring good health. Whether or not your believe this to be true, one thing, which can't be denied, is the feeling of relief accompanied by releasing a grudge or pent-up negativity. Holding a grudge against another person is often described as drinking poison and waiting for the other person to die.

Forgiveness, like gratitude for life's difficulties, is not for the weak. Forgiveness is an ability possessed by the powerful and the strong. It takes strong character to be able to forgive someone who you believe has wronged you. It takes equal courage to examine your own life and to learn to forgive yourself.

The long path to personal transformation is to continually work on your character bit by bit, piece by piece. However, there is a short cut. The short path is to force yourself, immediately, all at once, to forgive everyone who you believed has wronged you, starting with yourself. In doing so, your character is forged quickly and more powerfully. It is like overcoming a fear of heights. You can start by standing on a stool and, then, graduate to a ladder. Perhaps, next, you can look out the window of large building; then, you can go on a Ferris wheel, etc. Or, you could just skip all those steps and jump out of a plane three miles above the ground. Once you've done that, doing the other stuff becomes painless.

The same concept is true here; you can start by forgiving right now, by putting all your mental effort into forgiving everyone who you believe has ever wronged you. I am going to tell you how, in a moment. Once you have forgiven those people, you will have risen above the trivial stuff in life. Once you can forgive everyone you believe has ever wronged you, then, it's easier to apologize when you recognize that you've done something to upset or hurt another. You no longer hold onto grudges; you allow negative thoughts to quickly dissipate from your mind, and you increase the flow of positive energy through your body. That is the power of forgiveness.

Forgiveness also releases the victim mentality from your psyche; it restores your natural power to you. At first, it is not easy, though, with practice, it can be, and its rewards are worth much more than the effort it requires.

Forgiveness Exercise

Here is an exercise in forgiveness to begin at once. Set aside time in the morning or evening. If it is your first time doing this exercise, you may want to allow twenty to thirty minutes. Make a list of everyone you can think of, who you believe has wronged you. List everyone who you may be holding a grudge against. Include everyone who you think may have hurt you in the past. List everyone. Although you can do this mentally, whenever I do this exercise, I write everyone's name on a sheet of paper. I then read each name on the list, individually. I bring that person into my conscious mind, typically, by visualizing them, and, then, I say something like, "I forgive you. I wish all the best for you. I let you go." When doing this, say what feels right in your own heart, being sure to include the words, "I forgive you."

The first person on your list, and the first person you need to forgive, is yourself. Examine how you may be harboring anger towards yourself for a past behavior or circumstances. Realize that you, like everyone else, are doing the best you think you can at any given moment. Forgive yourself. Verbalize, "I forgive you." Feel the power of these words. Let them resonate through your being.

The next two people on your list are, typically, your parents. It is vital that you forgive your parents for anything you think they may have done wrong to you. In most cases, your parents were doing the best they could, from their vantage point. Try to see things from their perspective. Look on them with compassion, and, then, fully forgive you parents for anything you may feel bad about. Take pride in knowing that all of the circumstances of your life have benefited you in some way. You can't have the bad without the good. Be grateful for all of the good you have gained and which your parents, at the very least, have provided for in your life.

In my coaching, I have worked with people, who many decades later, hold anger against their parents for abuses they suffered as a child. This anger seems to plague their mind constantly, and it makes it difficult for them to lead fully functioning lives, in particular, to effectively parent their own children. When I speak with them about forgiveness, they respond by putting up much resistance; however, I explain to them that, by going through life with this animosity, it is akin to running a race with a parachute strapped to their back. In order to truly live, they have to let go. Otherwise the difficulties that they experienced as children never go away. Forgiveness is a powerful way to let go. To begin this process, I suggest to them to think of everything about their parents that they can be grateful for, at the very least, for having been born. By doing this, they start to change the energy of their thoughts. Then, the next step is to forgive and release the hold they've given their parents over their own mind. I repeat to them the following incantation: "Give thanks for the good; forgive the bad; release and let them go." Try repeating this phrase when you run up against resistance in your own practice. Realize, practicing forgiveness is not a one-time event. It is a very powerful practice, which you will want to repeat throughout your life, whenever you recognize that you are holding onto any anger towards another person.

Next, start with each additional person on your list, and think of all the benefits knowing them has provided you. Think of all the good things that have come as a result of the association. For example, in my own life, you would think that I might hold a grudge against Arnold, who bullied me in my youth. The opposite is actually true. So many benefits came from our knowing each other, even if his behavior towards me was contentious. Whenever I think of this person, I do so with gratitude. He was the catalyst that helped me to focus on improving my life, and he provided reasons for me to keep steadfast in pursuit of my goals.

For you, the person you hold a grudge against may be the same person that enabled you to become stronger or more independent, or to develop a better quality of yourself. In the Universe, you never get the bad without the good; the challenge is, you have to take the time to look for it. Once you've identified some of the good things that have occurred as a result of your association with this person, it becomes much easier to forgive the individual for any perceived wrongs you may be harboring grudges for towards them.

You never get the bad without the good.

Finally, the last step is to thank each of them in your mind for bringing the benefits you discovered to your awareness. Forgive them and let them go. Feel the energy release as you voice the words, "I forgive you and let you go." Then, move on to the next person and repeat. Typically, when I complete this exercise, I burn the entire list and mentally let everyone go.

Summary

Before you enter the spiritual realm through meditation and energy work, you must purify (make positive) your energy. (If you decide to expand your practice to include more esoteric activities, purifying your energy becomes even more important.) Practicing gratitude and forgiveness are the two fundamental ways to do this. Next, we will focus on developing a meditative practice to strengthen our spiritual connection and to enhance our peace of mind. Realize, meditation has no religious connotations, and practicing it doesn't require any specific belief system or allegiances. It is a tool every human is naturally equipped to make use of. It can be used to simply relax and relieve stress, or it can be used as a tool to awaken dormant faculties of the mind. It is a tool that can allow us to unfold, spiritually, while here on this planet. Nonetheless, it is a tool, which you decide how much you want to make use of, and how far you want to take it.

Meditation

In 1996, I began taking private lessons in Chi-Gung with an instructor I had learned about, after much research. I invited a friend to attend the private lessons, thinking this type of training would be of interest to him, as well, but my friend decided after the first lesson that it wasn't for him. Had I not had faith in the instructor's skill, I might have come to the same conclusion. Little did I know, what he had shown us in that first lesson were crucial pieces in the foundation of all energy systems, and, when practiced for a period of time, they would have a profound positive effect on my health. Nevertheless, at that moment, just after the first lesson, it didn't look like we had been exposed too much of anything. In fact, my friend later remarked, "I can't believe we just paid this guy to teach us how to breathe."

In that first lesson, the instructor taught us about a subject we were familiar with, called Chi, the Chinese word for the universal energy or life force that permeates all things (also called Ki in Japanese, Prana in Sanskrit, and energy in English). He explained, we can increase and store our Chi through concentration of our thoughts, refinement of our breath, and specific movements of our body. The more chi we harness, the more energy and life force we enjoy, and the greater our health and vitality, as well. To teach us how to cultivate more Chi, he started with the basics.

The first basic we learned was to rotate all of the joints in our body. By rotating our joints we bring Chi to that area. By bringing Chi to our joints, we potentially strengthen the joints, repair micro tears in ligaments and tendons, and remove energy blockages that can lead to pain and injury. In addition, we enliven our muscles and increase the flow of Chi throughout our body.

Here is a brief commentary on this first part of class: I later learned in studying Western medicine that there are receptors in the joints, and, when you rotate them in circles, they fire a signal to the muscles which makes the muscle more loose and flexible. In fact, ten years later, I could have probably avoided the torn tendon, if only I would have taken ten minutes to rotate my ankles, knees, and hips, before I rushed off down the terminal.

Currently, each morning and several times throughout the day, I rotate my joints, starting at my feet and working my way to my neck. I also have learned that regularly rotating the hip joints is especially good for men, for it increases healthy blood flow to the genital area.

Make joint rotation a regular part of your day. To do this, rotate each joint in a circle, first clockwise and then counter-clockwise, for multiples of nine. I typically aim for thirty-six rotations in each direction. When rotating your knees and hips, place your hands on your body, and concentrate on sending energy, through your hands, into your body. For optimum health, it is wise to rotate the joints each day, as well as stretch and exercise your muscles, daily. I will talk about this in more detail in the chapter on health.

The next thing we learned, which turned out to be one of the most valuable things I have ever been taught, was how to breathe properly. The first breath he taught us to perform is often referred to as the "Buddha's breath," "baby breath," or "belly breath." This is the way everyone should breathe, and it is the way a baby breathes before they grow into an adult and learn bad habits. To perform this breath is quite simple. Begin by inhaling, ideally through your nose, and, as you inhale expand your belly, focusing on expanding at the point four fingers length below your belly button (your center). Imagine, on the inhale, that you are pushing your stomach out and down. Next, as you naturally exhale, pull your stomach in at the same point, imagining you are bringing it to meet your spine. Practice this until it becomes natural.

Finally, the last part of the first lesson was an introduction to Chi-Gung standing meditation. In Chi-Gung, almost all of the meditations are active meditations. Active meditation is when your mind is given a specific focus for the meditation. In Chi-Gung, meditations typically involve combining rhythmic breathing with visualization to direct the flow of energy. Oftentimes, various body postures are combined with the breathing and the visualization as well. The other type of meditation is often referred to as passive meditation. Passive meditation, which is what I learned at the Dzogchen Buddhist center, is when you allow your mind to be still, and the only activity taking place is to notice the thoughts passing by but not to give any attention to them. Both of these types of meditation are valuable and provide a variety of benefits, ranging from reduction in blood pressure, to improved vitality and greater peace of mind. The peace of mind that is enjoyed is a result of the feeling that is developed through meditation, ideally that of being part of a greater whole. In addition, meditation has an amazing effect of lightening a troublesome thought or painful emotion. The practice of meditation seems to redirect the energy from the thought and returns that energy to the center of our being. The mental release that is typically experienced allows the practitioner to awaken from the meditation in a more resourceful, albeit relaxed, state of mind, in which to handle challenges and deal with circumstances. Once you have learned how to meditate, a powerful practice is to choose to meditate when feeling a negative emotion or wrestling with a challenge, as meditation is an excellent means for centering and transmuting negative energy to positive.

A Warrior of Life makes meditation a key part of his daily life. The meditation featured in this chapter combines both passive and active meditations into one cohesive session, which is intended to be performed each day as a daily spiritual ritual. The following are three of the best meditative practices I have learned, and they are meant to be used together, repeated daily.

The first component of the meditation is meant to relax the body and purposefully direct the flow of energy. The next part is designed to gain control of the mind and quiet the mental chatter, thus, improving the ability to focus and reducing the ceaseless flow of thoughts we experience daily (clear the mind). The third component is designed to create a state of total physical and mental relaxation. In this quiet space, you open your consciousness to the universe, allowing its expansive message to permeate your soul. Also, while in this state, the subconscious is more amendable to suggestion. To leverage this, we end the meditation with a brief period of visualizing our life's goals and intentions, as well as for affirmation, and prayer (prayer is used here to describe a communication with a higher power, not in a religious sense, and not by repeating specific rote phrases).

Warrior of Life Meditation

This is a seated meditation, and there are several options to choose from, when deciding which seated posture to use. The important thing is that you are seated, and not lying down. It is important for the flow of energy, as well as for your ability to maintain a meditative state without falling asleep, that you do not lie down or lean your back against anything to support you.

Although the practice of meditation, as performed in the East or by native tribes, is typically done in some sort of cross-legged seating position on the ground, the ancient Egyptian mystery schools performed meditation while seated on a chair. While training in a Chinese kung-fu system, which had a strong spiritual component, we would typically do active meditations, while seated in a chair. In Reiki, the attunements are performed while the receiver is seated in a chair (A Reiki attunement combines visualization and breathing, while in a meditative state, to channel the unique Reiki energies into the receiver). The chair is a very viable option, one that I personally recommend, especially, for those of you in the West, whose hips may not be as flexible. The choice between sitting in a chair or on the ground is not what's most important. Your ability to avoid distraction during the meditation, due to discomfort, is what matters.

If you decide to sit cross-legged on the floor, you will need to do so with the assistance of a cushion or zafu. The purpose of the cushion is to raise your hips off the ground, so they are above the knees, allowing for a balanced posture. It is not necessary to sit in a full-lotus position, unless it is comfortable for you. Even in that position, you typically must have a small cushion beneath your hips to support you in a balanced manner.

Once you have taken a seated position, the next step is to get comfortable in your space. I typically do this by moving my torso side to side, allowing my spine and sacrum to find that comfortable place where my body is in alignment, and held up naturally. Next, I roll my shoulders back to ensure that my back is in a natural, relaxed, balanced posture. Finally, I imagine that there is a piece of string connected to the top of my head (crown chakra), and it lifts my head up, causing my chin to tilt forward a little bit and causing my eyes to gaze just a few feet on the floor from where I am sitting. My hands I allow to rest in my lap, in some sort of a comfortable mudra (symbolic gesture in Hinduism and Buddhism typically done with the hands).

Choosing a mudra is important to me from the standpoint of developing an anchor. To facilitate your body's and mind's ability to get into a meditative state with ease, it is important to anchor the meditative experience in your mind and body. In this way, you are conditioning your mind to associate the mudra and the seated posture with the meditative state. The mudra I prefer is referred to as the "mountain mudra" in Tibet, and it is performed by resting your right hand in the palm of your left, with your thumbs touching each other, to create a seal.

Here are two additional suggestions to help you enter the meditative state quickly and with ease. The first is, to aim to meditate at the same time each day. Ideally, the morning is the best time to meditate to prepare your mind and body for the upcoming day. Also, you are not limited to just meditating in the morning; you can also meditate again at the end of the day or sometime during the day. You can, also, take mini-meditation breaks throughout the day, which we discuss in detail later. The next recommendation is, to meditate in the same spot each day. Find a place that is free from distraction, quiet, and appealing, in which to meditate each day. Begin to associate with this place in your mind as a place with a greater concentration of positive energy as a result of your meditating there daily. Make this an environment that fills you with energy, centers you, and increases your power for the day.

Once you have established a comfortable meditative posture, now you are ready to begin. What follows, is a recipe that I have developed from over fifteen years of study. It is one that combines cohesively, a variety of different meditative exercises, each of which could be performed independently from the rest, if you so desire. As your practice develops, you may come to favor a particular type of meditation, and you may choose to do it more often. Also, as you gain greater trust in your own intuition, you may choose to rely on intuitive promptings to choose, what method of meditation and what duration, is appropriate for that day's session.

To get started, make sure your tongue is placed lightly against the roof of your mouth directly behind your front teeth (this is very important). Close your eyes, and begin your meditation, by taking three complete "belly breaths," as taught earlier. First, we are going to relax the body. Starting at your feet, imagine them to be totally relaxed. Feel the tension completely leave them. Once you have this complete feeling of relaxation in your feet, move that feeling slowly up your legs, into your knees, into your hips, into your trunk, down and up your arms, into your neck, and up the back of your head and down your face, and then down the front of your body. Then, cycle this same relaxed feeling up the back of your body, starting at your feet, and down the front of your body, several more times.

Next, begin to feel this relaxed energy getting stronger, and begin circling it, first, starting at the base of your spine and, then, progressing up your back, over your head and down your face. Proceed down your chest and stomach, then, up your back again. This flow of energy is following a path that is called in Taoism, the *micro-cosmic orbit*. Following this orbit, energy travels up the back of the spine, and down the center of the chest and stomach. This orbit travels through each of the seven main chakras, beginning with the root chakra at the base of the spine, and travelling to the crown chakra at the top of the head.

Coordinate this flow of energy with your breath. Inhale the energy up your spine, and exhale it down your front. In other words, as you see the energy in your mind's eye, and feel the energy flowing, draw the energy up your back with a deep inhale of the breath, and then feel it cascade down the front of your body as you let out a slow, relaxing exhale of the breath.

As this energy orbits your body, feel it fully, as it travels up your spine, and down the center of your chest and stomach. Once you have done this for several complete cycles, then, visualize pooling the energy at your center (four finger lengths below your belly button). Then breathe a few breaths, specifically, to this point. You can store this energy by imagining it circling, first, clockwise, for thirty-six rotations and, then, counter-clockwise for twenty-seven, at the center of your body.

Next, we are going to clear the mind. On the next inhale, say to yourself, in your mind, the word, "Focus". This is a command to your mind. On the next exhale, say to yourself, in your mind, the number, "One." On the next inhale, say to yourself, in your mind, the word, "Relax." On the next exhale, say to yourself, in your mind, the number, "Two." Then, repeat the word, "Relax," on every inhale, and verbalize, in your mind, the next consecutive number on every exhale. Perform this process until you get to ten. If any other thought enters you mind and distracts you, momentarily, from your counting, simply begin the process again, starting over with the word, "Focus," and at the number one. Continue this active meditation, until you get to ten, without any other thought entering your mind. This will help condition your mind for meditation, and it will clear it, perhaps for a moment or more, of any latent thoughts.

Once you have completed the count, then, just sit. This type of sitting is often referred to as mindfulness meditation. This is the type of passive meditation we did at the Buddhist center. Ideally, you want to get to the point, where "sitting" makes up the bulk of your meditation session (this will become easier and your meditation, more efficient, with repetition). Continue breathing, and let your mind remain clear, for as long as you can, ideally, the rest of your meditation session. If a thought enters your mind, notice it, as if you were watching it cross a screen and then let it go. Don't attach to the thought.

Finally, always end a meditation session by visualizing and affirming, your goals and/or prayer (This will be explained more in Chapter Seven as part of the Daily Success Ritual). By visualizing your goals at this point, you are sending a direct message to your subconscious mind, saying, "This is what I want to manifest/experience in my life." This behavior will make sure that all your mental and spiritual faculties are on the lookout for ways to manifest these desires.

The total time to perform the Warrior of Life meditation should be between twenty to thirty minutes. I advocate that the majority of people should keep their meditation sessions to a maximum of thirty minutes. In the beginning of your practice, fifteen to twenty minutes should be more than sufficient.

This is the most powerful meditative practice I have found to help individuals experience the benefits of meditation rapidly, as well as to condition their minds for goal attainment. As you have seen, built into this practice is the harnessing and storing of Chi. Along with this is the quieting of the conscious mind of thoughts and the cultivating of the subconscious mind to be more receptive to our visualizations, affirmations and prayers. Do this daily for maximum benefit. It is not the amount of time you spend meditating per session that is beneficial, it's the cumulative power of meditation, as experienced by doing it every day. Only twenty minutes a day, performed every day, is better than an hour a day, performed three days a week.

Enough cannot be said about the power of meditation; however, the best way to understand this power, is to experience it for yourself. Make meditation a daily part of your life!

Additional Spiritual Practices

In addition to regular meditation, there are some additional ways to tend to your spiritual nature throughout each day. As I mentioned earlier, connecting to your Source is a very powerful way to develop serenity and peace of mind in your life. I also mentioned that the path to Spirit is through the mind, and a great practice is to fill the mind, daily, with words from spiritual texts. In my own library, I have the Bible, the Koran, the Bhagavad Gita, and the Tao Te Ching. In addition to traditional spiritual texts, like these, there are a variety of books available by Spiritual thought leaders. I have several books by the Dalai Lama, Thich Nhat Hanh, as well as Joel Osteen, Catherine Ponder, Eric Butterworth, Ernest Holmes, and many others. I recommend making books on Spirituality and living well an important part of your own personal library and daily reading.

Another way I connect with Spirit is by communing with nature. I enjoy meditating, while walking along the shore at the beach, sitting by a tranquil lake, hiking in the mountains, or just enjoying a leisurely walk through the woods. Try to schedule these types of activities into your life, as well, ideally, at least once a week. Perhaps it can be when you first wake up, during lunch hour at work, or maybe just on the weekends, at first. The important thing is that you make tending to your Spirit a priority, and you set aside this time for yourself.

Also, practice mini-meditations throughout the day. You can perform one of the components of the Warrior of Life meditation, such as counting the breath, or circling energy through the micro-cosmic orbit, for a few minutes, several times throughout the day. Or you can simply set a clock for five minutes and sit, simply noticing your thoughts and not attaching to them. The breathing is what will make this most effective. The essence of all meditation can be found in the breath. Deep breathing is good for the body, good for the mind, and great for the soul. Meditate on this.

Lastly, practice the tenets these books speak about in your daily life. Practice happiness, detachment, forgiveness, understanding, gratitude, and let your actions be a positive example for others. It's unwise to practice spirituality and meditate in the morning, only to lose your temper while driving to the office, because you perceived someone intentionally cut you off.

Chapter Summary

Spiritual practices such as those presented in this chapter possess a cumulative power. The more you practice them, the more your own spiritual powers begin to grow, culminating in greater awareness, peace of mind, and appreciation, to name just a few. Through gratitude and forgiveness, you are able to develop stronger relationships and greater connectedness with others. Through meditation you allow yourself to connect to that indescribable power--often referred to as God, Source, Spirit, and Nature--on a regular basis. Through this connectedness, other spiritual attributes, such as detachment, giving, service, and love, seem to naturally unfold. To experience all of these blessings, commit yourself to your daily spiritual practice. Use this book as a guide, and use your journal as a resource to track your growth.

Action Steps:

1. Practice gratitude, daily, by writing down, each day, five things for which you are grateful.
2. Do the forgiveness exercises presented in this book.
3. Take time throughout the day to practice the "Buddha breath". Do ten deep cleansing Buddha breaths, at least three times per day.
4. Meditate for at least twenty minutes, once per day. Eventually expand your practice to thirty minutes, once or twice per day.
5. Spend time in nature. Perhaps, go outside to read the next chapter of this book.

Chapter Five

Warrior of Life Mind Training

-White Belt and Green Belt-

The Warrior of Life program is very much a mental development program. A Warrior of Life is someone, who embraces the challenge of taking control of his mind, eliminating the limiting thoughts and beliefs that are keeping him from living the life he desires. He analyzes his thoughts, regularly, removing the negative and replacing them with the positive. Since a belief is simply a persistent thought, by examining his reoccurring thoughts and changing those which are limiting, the changing of beliefs, from limiting to empowering, takes care of itself.

A Warrior of Life is a positive thinker and is solution-oriented. He entertains positive thoughts and expectations, and he remains vigilant to prevent negative thinking from taking root in his mind. In doing this, he enjoys greater happiness, well-being, and peace of mind. He is able to live a much fuller, richer life, accomplishing things others only dream about.

You have already read about some of the mental techniques and philosophies that make up the Warrior of Life program, such as "long term thinking" and "personal success rules." In this chapter, we will take a more direct and systemized approach, starting with the basics and expanding. To do this, we will borrow a framework from martial arts, which is the belt ranking system. In the martial arts, the belt ranking system serves several purposes. As mentioned earlier, the first is that it teaches the essence of, and mechanics of, goal setting. It teaches students how to achieve a major goal, such as earning a black belt, by breaking it down into smaller, but still progressive, goals, which are the lesser belt ranks. Starting with the white belt, the student progresses to various colors, which signify achievement, after demonstrating the equivalent mastery of the techniques associated with each belt rank. Ultimately, the student arrives at the rank of black belt, possessing all of the knowledge and qualities of a black belt.

In the martial arts, a black belt denotes someone who has demonstrated commitment and proficiency, in all of the basic techniques which form a particular martial arts system. By mastering these techniques, he is now ready for advanced training, which could only be attempted by someone who had mastered the basics. By demonstrating this commitment in mastering the basics, the black belt organically develops the qualities of discipline and persistence, which expand cumulatively, allowing him to develop abilities far beyond that of the average person.

Developing yourself is a never-ending, progressive endeavor. As a metaphor for achievement, to get you started in the right direction, I have associated the key mental techniques, philosophies, and strategies, forming this program with an equivalent belt rank, progressing all the way to black belt.

White Belt

The first belt is the White Belt, and it represents the beginner's mind. The beginner's mind is something that should be cultivated throughout one's life. To look at everything with a beginner's mind provides a unique and fresh perspective. This is invaluable in business, whether in research and development, manufacturing, sales, or marketing. To be constantly learning, to be free from the trappings of ego and open to the fact that everyone has something of value to offer, is the essence of the beginner's mind. Even the black belt encompasses this quality, for, just as with any goal in life, when a student reaches the black belt, they find they are standing at the beginning of yet another journey.

Do you approach life with a beginner's mind?

In the martial arts there is a story that teaches the importance of a beginner's mind. In the story, an arrogant young swordsman comes to learn from a master swordsman the way of the master's system. However, when the student arrives, the master is not able to get a word in, for he is constantly interrupted by the student prognosticating his own exploits and ideas. The master, then, invites the young swordsman to join him over a cup of tea. As the young man keeps talking about his own philosophies, the master pours him tea, and continues to pour after the cup is full, forcing the tea to run over. Startled, the young swordsman points this out to the master, to which the master replies, "Until you empty your own cup, you can't receive any more tea."

I mentioned in the first chapter that one of the things I admired about Mike Trimarchi, my first martial arts instructor, was that he was always open to learning new skills. Here is someone who is always emptying his cup, and this is what has allowed him to continually grow and advance. Jim Rohn, the famous motivational speaker, who is acknowledged to have been a mentor of Tony Robbins, once, described Tony's insatiable thirst for knowledge as being the dominating quality that made his success so remarkable. In my opinion, Tony is another positive example of someone who is often emptying his cup, and approaching new fields and new areas of study, with a beginner's mind.

Following in the footsteps of the masters, please empty your cup, and allow yourself to drink up all the insights and essential power contained in the following principles and techniques.

Kaizen

Kaizen is the first white belt technique. Kaizen is a Japanese word that means constant and never-ending improvement. This principle can be applied to almost any aspect of life, from personal development to building a successful company. Kaizen is best applied by making small daily improvements in the key areas of your life. Kaizen is a principle that you can make use of to tackle a major goal or project, by breaking the goal down it down into smaller pieces and, then, building upon those pieces, until it is complete. With this approach, eventually, almost any goal can be realized.

Kaizen is the principle that will make it possible, for anyone, to make this program a part of their life, regardless of the challenge. For example, you've learned about the importance of daily meditation; however, you may be thinking that you don't have the time or the energy to commit yourself to twenty minutes of meditation, each day. Perhaps, you have the excuse that you can't sit for that long; well, you can apply Kaizen by deciding to meditate each day, initially only for a minute. Then, you may find that you can go for two minutes. Soon, you're sitting for five or ten minutes. Before you know it, enough time has passed; you've built up the discipline, and, now, you are meditating for thirty minutes. That is the power of Kaizen, and it can be applied to any aspect of your life.

Perhaps, you are not exercising each day as you know you should, for your good health. Using this same principle, you can decide to exercise for a minute. What can you do in minute, you ask? You can do, at least, ten pushups, ten squats, and/or ten sit-ups. Do this, every day, for a week. The following week, add another minute. Just as with meditation, the important thing is not bulk of time, it's consistency. This is worth repeating. *The important thing is consistency.* Two minutes a day, every day, will do more for you, mentally and physically, than thirty minutes, once a week.

Apply Kaizen in your financial life. Suppose you know that you should be saving ten percent of your income, but you have excuses and limiting beliefs of why that is not possible for you. Start, now, by saving only one percent. Save a penny from every dollar you earn. How easy is that, just one penny from every dollar? It doesn't matter the amount; it matters the consistency. By applying Kaizen, you are creating new, more empowering habits, while eliminating negative habits and behaviors. With every instance, you are turning towards what you desire to experience more of in your life. As in this example, by saving one penny from every dollar, you go from a person who doesn't save, to a person who does save. It's the same with exercise; even if you only exercise for a minute a day, in your mind you are transforming from a person who doesn't exercise, to a person who does. This shift in your mind, and in your life, can make all the difference in determining your future decisions and actions--and the direction they take your life.

Take a moment now to determine what some improvements would be in your behavior that you might have been putting off because it appeared to require too much effort or time. Apply the principle of Kaizen to make those changes now. Take a step in the direction of your goals. Any step, even a small step, can have a measurable impact over time. The key to success is movement; in other words, the key to success, in any area of life, is consistent action in the direction of your goals. Consistent actions, even weak ones, at first, will lead to explosive growth and change in the long run. That is the essence of Kaizen.

Substitution Principle

During my sophomore year of college, I was inspired to get serious about improving my health and fitness. I had learned from books such as those by Brian Tracy and Stephen Covey how important habits were, and that it takes roughly 21 days to change/develop a new habit. The first area of my health I wanted to improve was my nutrition, and the first habit I decided to change was my daily habit of drinking a soft drink. Up to that point, every afternoon in between classes, I would reach for a soda. I had learned in my reading that *all of nature abhors a vacuum*, and that if I didn't find something to replace the soda with, I would either continue to reach for it or grab something else, which might be worse. I had read about the substitution principle in books on nutrition, and I decided to give it a try. I substituted iced tea in place of the soda (eventually I just decided to drink mostly water, some tea, and an occasional coffee); this worked like a charm, and I decided to use the approach again. For instance, up until that point, every morning, on the way to a health class, I would grab something out of the vending machine. Usually it was a sugary, high-fat, processed pastry or a candy bar (really good to arrive with these things at health class). I realized that this behavior wasn't consistent with the new health and nutrition habits I wanted to develop, so I decided I would substitute a banana. Every day, for the rest of the semester, I would eat a banana. I only decided to change to an apple, after one day, when the professor asked if she could use the banana, as a prop to teach students the proper way to apply a condom.

The substitution principle made perfect sense to me, and it worked in changing a variety of habits. For example, I'd substitute a book instead of TV, an apple instead of a donut, and water instead of a soft drink. Then, one day, I discovered that the substitution principle was one of the most powerful methods for developing the mind, as well. I learned that the substitution principle is the tool the Tibetan Yogis use to develop seemingly supernatural mind powers. They do this by paying attention to their thoughts. First, they pick a thought that crosses their mind, and then they decide to substitute a better thought in its place. They repeat the better thought like a mantra until it takes hold in their mind. Through this process, they continue to build their mental powers by improving the quality of each individual thought.

To use the substitution principle in your mind, you have to accept the fact and responsibility that your mind is the one thing that is completely under your control. For example, here in the United States, we have many freedoms, but, the truth is, freedom can be taken from anyone in the form of loss of liberties. However, the one freedom that everyone possesses is freedom over their own mind, and this can never be taken away from you, without you allowing it. Unfortunately, too many people don't exercise this freedom in a constructive way by taking positive control over the thoughts that they allow to reside in their mind. The thoughts they harbor are a result of the negative news they may hear on the radio, the worries and complaints emanating from the people around them, and the past negative conditioning that has a jaded effect on how they interpret new events in their life. You can change all that through the ideas in this book, starting with the substitution principle.

The best way to use the substitution principle on your mind is to pay attention to the thoughts you are thinking and, deliberately, substitute a positive thought for any negative thought. When you catch yourself thinking a negative thought, quickly replace it by substituting a positive thought of your choosing. Typically, the opposite of the negative thought is the best substitution. Then, dwell on the positive thought. Do this, and, eventually, your mind will be filled with positive, empowering thoughts. Since thoughts lead to action, which leads to results, surely enough, this is the fastest way to manifest the life of your dreams.

When I ran my first marathon, I had the chance to practice this principle while running 26.2 miles. Since it was my first marathon, initially, some of the thoughts I had were worrisome, such as, "What if I can't finish?" To manage this thought, I identified what I perceived was its opposite, and I started repeating, "I am easily completing this marathon." I pictured myself, over and over in my mind, crossing the finish line. Later on, I had thoughts that were encouraging me to take a break, or to walk for a while. As soon as I caught myself entertaining these thoughts, I immediately substituted some of my own. I remember that one of the thoughts I started chanting to myself was, "I can do it." It's amazing how a simple phrase, such as "I can do it," can have such a powerful, positive effect on performance. This thought alone, and others like it, propelled me the entire length of the course and over the finish line. They continue to propel me in other areas of my life to this day.

Momentum Technique

Momentum is something you intentionally make use of to achieve your goals. The key to making momentum technique work for you is simply to choose a goal, and take immediate action. Once you get the momentum going, through action, it picks up additional intensity, of its own accord, to help propel you forward, in the direction of your intention.

For instance, when you set a new goal, the key to manifesting that goal, is, immediately, to begin moving towards its manifestation. As you move towards the goal by taking action, each action builds on the preceding, gaining the crucial momentum, which helps propel you forward. This is worth repeating: the best way to gain momentum is to decide to take an action, immediately after setting a new goal. This is key! Whenever you set a goal, immediately take some action towards its achievement. As we learned with Kaizen, even the smallest actions, if repeated daily, will eventually lead to large rewards.

Momentum technique is very powerful, and it works in concert with both Kaizen and the substitution principle. For example, you set a goal to lose ten pounds of weight. You decide immediately to stop your habit of watching TV upon arriving home for work, and you choose to substitute exercise to fill the vacuum of time. So, when you arrive home, you immediately gain additional momentum by going out for a short run. You then repeat the run each day, improving (Kaizen) in stamina and fitness, until running has become a habitual part of your behavior. Ideally, the momentum from your new running program, which shows up in a variety of ways, inspires you to improve your nutrition. Once you set the goal to improve your nutrition, you gain momentum by immediately throwing away all the junk food from your cabinets. Next, you identify areas where you can substitute healthy options for less healthy options. This continues to grow and grow, until eventually these positive habits fill your life. That is the power of gaining momentum towards achieving your goals.

Discipline

As a child, I used to fantasize about having superpowers, like those possessed by comic book heroes, such as Superman. I would often imagine the advantages these powers would provide me. Many years later, I discovered that there was such a superpower, and it was available to me. In fact, it is available to all of us, but it is typically cultivated only by a certain few. With this power, a human being could develop himself to the point of accomplishing, seemingly, super human feats. The superpower I discovered is discipline.

Discipline is the power to get yourself to do the things, which you know you must do, in order to achieve your goals. Applying discipline in your life requires making use of your will and your personal energy. The ability to make use of discipline in your life by focusing your will and harnessing your energy is often referred to as your *personal power*. That is what this book is also really about, building and strengthening your personal power.

When you hear the word Warrior you probably think of someone who is powerful. By applying the techniques in this book, and making them a part of your life, you are exercising your discipline and increasing your power. With this power, you become the type of person who can accomplish whatever he sets his mind to. By the way, discipline is what makes applying every one of these mental techniques possible. Different from momentum and substitution, discipline is a quality which needs to be purposefully cultivated. Discipline is built just like a muscle in your body. For example, the more you exercise the muscle, the stronger the muscle gets. The same is true with discipline. The more you practice discipline in the many facets of your life, the stronger becomes your ability to apply discipline. On the other hand, each time you fail to do the things that you know you need to do, your discipline weakens.

When embarking on a developing a new habit, such as starting an exercise program, for example, the force of inertia is working against you. To gain momentum, you need to harness your energy and focus your will on the task at hand. This is where your level of discipline comes in, and why it is important to be constantly developing this power. With a strong level of discipline you can get yourself to commit yourself to this new habit and, ultimately, achieve your goal.

To develop your personal power of discipline, begin today by applying the techniques you are learning in your daily life. To get yourself started, answer the following questions: What is one thing, which you know you should do, but you have been putting off? What is one small step that you could take, right now, to begin gaining momentum towards a particular goal? Do the thing, now.

What is one behavior or habit that you know you should change? Is it watching mindless TV on the "killer couch" for several hours each day? Is it eating unhealthy snacks during the day? Is it spending money on mundane purchases to fill gaps in your time? Once you identify it, ask yourself, what is a healthy behavior, which you can substitute in its place, right now? Do the thing now.

These techniques are a part of the exact strategies that I used to begin transforming my life. I've mentioned, already, how I substituted a banana for a candy bar, and tea for soda. Once I gained momentum, I started examining all of the areas of my life where I could apply these principles. I began listening to audio books in the car instead of the radio. I would read instead of watching TV. I would discipline myself to get up an hour early to meditate in the morning, instead of just lying in bed. I would walk instead of taking the elevator. I would bike instead of driving to school. That is the power of discipline combined with substitution and momentum in action, and all of these things brought me closer, each day, to becoming the person I intended, and achieving the vision I had for myself (kaizen). The same, and more, can be true for you!

Green Belt

The next belt is the Green Belt. At this level, you begin to move away from average. Through disciplined application of the previous mental techniques you are already beginning to separate yourself from average thinking and you are becoming more powerful. You are doing things that the average person doesn't do, or isn't willing to do. You are earning a spot among those rare individuals, who desire more of themselves and of life, and who are willing to pay the price to achieve this.

Next, you are going to be introduced to mental techniques that are diametrically opposite to the way the average person looks at things. Through effort, you can make these your own, and you can experience the commensurate benefits that this effort produces.

Solution Thinking

The average person goes out of their way to avoid problems. Instead of meeting a problem head-on, he will turn away from it, hoping it will go away. Worse, still, he will dwell on the problem itself, worrying about the problem, sharing the problem with anyone who will listen, later on, wondering why he continues to be plagued by similar problems. I have a family member, who, whenever something he deems bad happens to him, he tells anyone who will listen about his most recent troubles. Put him in a gathering of people, and, by the end of the night, he has recounted his troubling story twenty times. Apparently, he doesn't realize that, with each telling, he is building negative thoughts, negative feelings, and negative energy in his body. Over time, this will have a cataclysmic effect on his health and his peace of mind. Don't let this be you.

A Warrior of Life takes a different approach to difficult situations and problems. He realizes that, hidden within every problem, there is a benefit. The late Napoleon Hill, author of such books as *Think and Grow Rich* and *Your Magic Key to Riches* said it best, "Hidden within every adversity is the seed to an equal or greater benefit."

In Japanese, the kanji (language symbol) for problem is, also, the kanji for opportunity. Your problems represent the best opportunities for your growth. This is worth repeating. Your problems represent the best opportunities for your growth. In order to transform these problems, the Warrior of Life must adjust the lens in which he views his problems to see them as challenges to be met, and opportunities to be enjoyed.

The first step to turn a problem into an opportunity is to begin by changing the wording we use, which I will refer to as our "warrior vocabulary" (this brings up an a good time to share the following maxim for success: The level of our success in life will be determined by how we communicate with ourselves, and with other people. In this section we are mostly working on how we communicate with ourselves, though, communicating in this way to your spouse or colleagues is advantageous as well). From now on, refer to anything you deem to be a problem as a challenge. The word challenge inherently brings about different feelings than the word problem. Most people agree that a challenge can be good and worthwhile. For this reason, substitute the word challenge for the word problem when speaking to others and in your own mind.

Next, it is important to reframe the perspective we have on how problems fit into our lives. Look at it this way: Problems present opportunities for growth. People who solve problems are people who are growing. In the workplace, problem solvers, typically, earn more money and are looked upon for leadership opportunities. In fact, the best way to get ahead at work is to determine what problems may be plaguing your department or company, reframe them as challenges, and then go to work looking for solutions. Present these solutions to your boss and you will have completely separated yourself from your peers.

Finally, once you've reframed the problem in your mind as a challenge and, therefore, a potential opportunity, do *not* think about, talk about, or focus on the problem; rather, focus on possible solutions. This approach refers to two things we learned earlier. What we think about or focus on, we attract more of, due to the universal Law of Attraction. If you focus your mind on finding possible solutions, your reticular cortex will be on the lookout for solutions to your challenges, and the Universe will put solutions in your path. Secondly, your subconscious mind, and all its resources, can be put to use to help you find a solution. As mentioned earlier, one of the most effective ways to activate your subconscious mind is to pose the challenge in the form of a question: "How can I solve...?", "What is the best way to…?", "How can I (earn, grow, improve, change, obtain)?", for example.

Focus on Solutions, Avoid Distractions

When I decided to learn to skydive, I signed up for a program called Accelerated Free Fall (AFF). AFF combined eight skydiving lessons/jumps with an additional twelve semi-supervised jumps, to help qualify a student to become a licensed skydiver with the United States Parachute Association. My first lesson consisted of four to six hours of ground school, where I learned the fundamentals of freefall and, most importantly, how to pilot a parachute, safely, to the ground. Different from a tandem skydive, where the instructor is connected to you for the entire skydive, the first AFF skydive begins with you exiting the plane at a high altitude (typically 14,500 feet above the ground), held by two instructors. At the appropriate altitude during the freefall, the instructors let you go as you pull your parachute. You then follow a pre-determined flight plan back to the drop zone landing area. As you get closer and within view, the instructor actually gives you landing commands via a two-way walkie-talkie, stored conveniently in the sleeve pocket of your upper left arm, on your flight suit. My first skydive went off without a hitch. It was exhilarating! I adequately performed all the basic maneuvers associated with the first level. I, then, pulled my parachute and successfully landed on target at the drop zone. However, my second jump didn't go as planned, but from this experience I had deeply implanted in my psyche, the power of solution thinking.

On my second skydive, we exited the plane further away from the landing area than planned, due to cloud cover. The simple remedy was for me to pull my parachute at a higher altitude; however, I misread my instructor's non-verbal command, and I ended up pulling it at a lower altitude than the one he intended. It didn't take me long to realize that I was not going to make it back to the drop zone. Immediately, all the potential things that could go wrong, started flashing through my mind, and, needless to say, I was not in a very powerful state of mind; however, the next thing that happened completely changed my focus and my state. It ultimately led me to finding a safe place to land. One of the instructors had landed close enough to the vicinity where I was flying my parachute, although we couldn't see each other. He radioed to me via the walkie-talkie these words, which I would barely have been able to make out due to static, had he not repeated them with intensity, several times. He said, "Find a field to land in; avoid power lines...find a field to land in; avoid power lines." Upon hearing these commands, my focus changed. I was no longer focusing on the problem, and all the things that could go wrong; instead, I gave my mind one simple thing to focus on which was to find a field to land in, while avoiding power lines. Fortunately, I found a safe field to land in, and have to admit, I thoroughly enjoyed my little adventure. Plus, I turned his commands (with a slight adjustment) into a maxim for problem solving, applicable to everyday life, which is, "Focus on the solution; avoid distractions."

Focus on the solution; avoid distractions.

When you are focused on the solution instead of the problem, you feel better, you think better, and you are in a more resourceful state. Whatever challenges you are currently faced with, focus on finding a solution, and don't dwell on the problem. The solution may be not be something so general as finding the right field to land in, but, the more you look in that general direction, the more likely it is that you will discover the right solution for you.

Lastly, an empowering concept to understand is that your goals--the goals you set for yourself to achieve--are also challenges. Your goals are challenges waiting for you to solve them. A goal is something that you can't achieve with your current level of ability and resources. A good goal forces you to become better, in order to achieve it. If you can achieve the goal simply with the money, skills, and resources you have now, then it is not a goal, and it is probably not very challenging. For example, if you have goal to earn a specific amount of money, well beyond what you are currently earning, that is a challenge. By focusing on the solution – earning the larger income – you invoke the power of your subconscious mind, and the law of attraction, in bringing ideas into your conscious purview. Once you identify ideas that resonate with you, the next step is the easy one; take the action. (We will discuss challenges in greater detail in chapter nine).

At the following rank of Blue Belt, I will discuss affirmations and making them a part of your daily life. One great way to activate the power of an affirmation, in order to solve a challenge, is to pose it as a question to your subconscious. Your subconscious mind will then go to work to find the answer.

Inverse Thinking

Inverse thinking can be applied when solving challenges and/or changing behaviors. Inverse thinking simply means to think the opposite. To apply inverse thinking, take the situation that is causing you frustration or the challenge you are dealing with, and make its opposite your goal.

Inverse thinking also involves doing the opposite of the unsuccessful people. Since our thoughts ultimately lead to our actions, by focusing on doing the opposite of unsuccessful individuals, we will perform differently, as well. Inverse thinking doesn't require that you do the complete opposite, but, rather, that you *do more of one thing and less of another*. For example, the average person spends too much time sitting on the "killer couch," watching the "plug-in drug". According to studies, the average household has the television on seven to eight hours a day. Apply inverse thinking by changing that in your own household. Do the things that other people won't do. For example, instead of watching TV, read a book. Spend time with your family, go to the gym or some other exercise, or work on a side business. Visit a museum or meditate. This doesn't mean you must give up TV entirely; just watch it much less.

In addition, if you notice the unsuccessful person showing up late for work and leaving early, do the opposite, by showing up early and leaving late. A common trait among all successful people I know and have read about, is the habit of arriving to work early. By the way, in his book *Automatic Wealth*, Michael Masterson says, "Getting to work early is such a common virtue of successful people, that I'm tempted to call it the single most important thing that you can do to change your life."

If the unsuccessful person is eating fast food for lunch each day, bring a healthy lunch from home. If the unsuccessful person spends their nights at happy hour, create your own happy hour with your family doing quality activities. I often spend my own "happy hour" on Friday evenings, running several miles, to kick-off the weekend. I fire up my metabolism, and I shake off the stresses of the week, to get in the right frame of mind to make the most of my weekend with my family. That is the power of how inverse thinking leads to successful actions. Write down, in your Warrior of Life journal, ways you can apply inverse thinking in your own life, now. Gain momentum by taking some action, now.

Positive Thinking

Norman Vincent Peale is the late author of the highly successful book *The Power of Positive Thinking*, a book which helped lift the masses out of the mental despair of the Great Depression. He is often paraphrased as saying that 76% of a man's thoughts are negative, and by changing the balance of negative thoughts to positive thoughts, such a man can accomplish things that others could barely dream of.

Even with 76% of his thoughts being negative in nature--meaning they are pessimistic, "glass half-empty," worrisome, problem-focused thoughts-- the average person still leads a decent life. Now imagine, if you could tip the scales to where over 50% of your thoughts were positive--optimistic, "glass half-full," excited, and filled with positive-expectancy, solution-focused thoughts--what amazing things you could then accomplish! People would be attracted to you; opportunities would present themselves; your energy would rise, and your motivation would greatly increase. All this would happen because you put effort into changing the nature of your thoughts.

In the martial arts, the mind is often thought of as a garden. In a garden, what you plant in the soil will eventually grow in the garden. In addition, weeds will grow on their own and strangle the vegetables and fruits you plant, if you are not vigilant in eliminating them. The gardener must do these two things: plant what he wants to grow, and be vigilant to remove the weeds. Just like the garden, whatever thoughts you plant in your mind will grow, and they will, eventually, show up in your experience. Plant positive thoughts and you will reap positive results. On the other hand, if you allow negative thoughts to enter and grow in the garden of your mind, eventually, these weeds will take over the garden, and negativity will abound in your attitude. It will eventually enter your relationships, your work, and all other areas of your life. The key is, to purposefully plant (namely, through affirmation, reframing, and positive thinking) positive thoughts, and to be vigilant not to allow even a single negative thought to enter the mind. The strategies in this book will help you in a variety of ways. By regularly meditating, you are learning to calm and focus your mind. This will allow you to become more aware of your thinking and notice your thoughts. Apply the substitution principle in your mind, whenever you catch yourself thinking one negative thought. This is the aforementioned technique the Tibetan Yogis utilize. Immediately, replace a negative thought with a positive one, and affirm this positive thought multiple times mentally and/or verbally, to help it take root. We will talk more about this in the section on affirmations. Another thing you can do is to wear an elastic band on your wrist, and, any time you catch yourself thinking a negative thought, snap the band. Eventually, your mind will become conditioned to think mainly positive thoughts. This is vitally important, for the key to mental strength is controlling your mind, to the point that you don't even entertain a negative thought. Eventually, it's as if you are surrounded by a force field that prevents negative people and circumstances from penetrating or upsetting your serene mind. Furthermore, it has been my experience that negative, complaining people typically steer clear of positive, focused, powerful individuals.

In working with and studying many successful individuals, from all walks of life, I have found that, most of the successful people I've met, typically, use a different language than those who are struggling in life. I believe it is because these successful individuals realize the power of cultivating a positive attitude, and they understand that it begins with harboring positive thoughts. Their attitude is reinforced by conditioning themselves, habitually, to say positive words and phrases. You, too, can use the power of your words and language to create the life you desire to lead; the recipe is contained throughout this book.

Another aspect of positive thinking is positive expectation. Positive expectation and optimism go hand in hand. It is expecting the best from yourself, and from other people. It's expecting to succeed, to do well, to complete what you start, and to achieve your goals. One way to apply positive expectation in your daily life is to decide in advance, before any activity you engage in, the desired outcome for that activity. On your way to work, expect to have a great day. Before a meeting, expect things to go well. Even before a workout, expect your body to perform at its best. Cultivate positive expectation in every endeavor you engage in. The mystics teach us that everything we see and experience is a projection of our own minds. Though it may sound like the stuff of fantasy, western scientists, through the work of noted physicists in the fields of quantum science, are proving the same things. If this is true (which it is), going into a segment of your day by mentally deciding what you intend to, or expect to, occur is a powerful way to create your world in the present moment. This, as with all the other principles, becomes easier to apply with practice. So, take a moment before any segment of your day, whether it's a meeting, presentation, workout, dinner with a spouse, playing with the kids, etc., and decide in advance how good you want that time to be, and what positive experiences you expect to manifest.

One last aspect of positive thinking, utilized by the Warrior of Life, is called mental projection. Mental projection begins with the self. By changing your thoughts in relation to others, you can affect the other person's behavior towards you. For example, I was taught a very esoteric self-defense technique involving mental projection. Imagine you are walking in a strange city, and you see three people walking towards you, whose body language indicate that they may be trouble (the real masters would recognize trouble by sensing the negative energy vibration projected from their auras, but reading body language is a good place to start). Immediately respond by visualizing, in your mind, what physical response you will take to deal with them, if they act on their nefarious intentions. Visualize, with intensity, the level of violence you will inflict on them in response, if they try to do you harm. By visualizing this, the following things seemingly take place: first, it would have an effect on your body language, which would indicate you are not one to be messed with; second, it would change your energy vibration, sending out a vibe that you are not one to be messed with; finally, just as a radio signal travels through the ether, it is possible they might get a sense of your thoughts, encouraging them to respond wisely by not giving you trouble (there is an advanced version, where you mentally project that you are someone to help, which doesn't require visualizing a physical response).

Mental projection is not limited just to self-defense. It can be applied in many areas of your life, from asking out the guy or girl you like, to making a successful sales call. Like all things, to apply mental projection begins with how you communicate with yourself, and the best way is to start by changing your vocabulary, using the inverse thinking technique.

Instead of thinking, "What if he or she says no?"
Ask, "What if he or she says yes?"

Instead of thinking (on a sales call), "What if they say no?"
Ask, "What if they say yes?"

Instead of thinking "What if it doesn't work?"
Ask, "What if it works?"

Instead of thinking "What if I fail?"
Ask, "What if I succeed?"

Instead of thinking "What will I lose?"
Ask, "What can I gain?"

Instead of thinking "I have to do this."
Say, "I get to do this."

Instead of thinking "Will they like me?
Ask, "Will I like them?"

Once you start thinking the inverse, and harboring this positive version of it in your mind, you approach the situation from a more empowered position, allowing the universe to match up circumstances with your thinking.

Next, before we move onto the Blue Belt techniques, we are going to take a break to do a Goal Setting Workshop. With your goals clearly identified, we will move on to the next series of techniques, designed to firmly implant them into your subconscious mind, allowing for their natural unfolding.

Action Steps:

1. What is one thing, which you know you should do, but you have been putting off? What is one small step that you could take, right now, to begin gaining momentum towards a particular goal? Do the thing, now.

2. Sit down, with a pad and pen, and try to identify all the benefits contained within the challenges that you are currently facing. Really search for the benefit. Once you've identified it, take a small action towards realizing that benefit in your life.

3. What are some of the distractions in your life, currently taking your focus off your goals, e.g. TV, procrastination, task items that lack urgency and importance but gain your attention? What can you substitute in their places?

4. Pick a positive phrase that resonates with you, write it down, and place it somewhere where you can see it, often. Repeat it throughout the day.

Chapter 6

Goal Setting Workshop

Goals are an essential to living a full rewarding life, and, as humans, we have been naturally programmed with goal achievement software. Our abilities to decide, visualize, focus, attract, and act, are just some parts of the natural goal achievement programming, which comes already installed, when we are born into this life. The desire for things is, also, something that is a natural part of us, as well. The desire for things is not something that we have to be taught; in fact, in most cases, unfortunately, the opposite is true. Typically, as children, we are constantly being told our limitations, as opposed to what's possible.

I define goals simply as "desires with deadlines." The word *desire* comes from the Latin root de-sire, meaning "of the spirit". Interestingly, the ancient masters tell us that we are actually spirit, here on earth to have a human experience. This means that your spirit, the authentic you, is helping to guide the ship. This also means that our goals, and the ability to achieve them, are also spiritual in nature.

As a spiritual being on earth, at this time having a human experience, please take a moment to realize that all of your desires, anything you desire to be, to do, or to have, is your spirit seeking greater expression and greater experience of physical life, here, on this planet, at this time. When you have a desire to be more, do more, or have more, this desire is brought into your conscious awareness, from that part of you, which is eternal and connected to all things. This means that, essentially, all of our desires to expand and grow are derived from Spirit. It is spiritual to want more health. It is spiritual to want deeper relationships. It is spiritual to want more money. It is spiritual to want to enjoy more places, more toys, more meals, more books, and more things. Of course, I don't have to tell you that it is also very spiritual to want to give, share, help, and make a positive difference in the lives of others. As mentioned in the first paragraph of this chapter, the ability to manifest all of your desires is inborn, and it is a natural part of you.

There is a law in nature that says," If you are not growing, then you are dying." If you are not expanding, then you are shrinking. You are here to expand, to grow, to become more, and that is what goals do for you. The famous speaker and teacher Jim Rohn said, "The reason to set a goal is not for what you will get. The reason to set a goal is for what you will become." You set goals to grow, to become better, and to see what achieving the goal can make you as a person. Through the journey of continually moving from where you are, towards where you want to be, you experience the fullness of life and grow into the manifestation of the unlimited powerful person you truly are.

Efficient Effort

If, up to this point, you have been making excuses or harboring limited beliefs about why you can't have what you want, don't do that anymore. It is all an illusion anyway, a trick of a poorly conditioned mind. You can have anything you desire, to the degree that you are willing to offer the equivalent amount of your personal focus, energy, and activity (called effort). I define effort as the combination of focus, energy, and activity. A Warrior of Life understands that there is no such thing as something for nothing in the Universe; the goals you set for yourself will require varying degrees of effort to manifest them. Effort is a beautiful thing, for you can't put effort into something without getting something positive back. The more effort you put into something, the more benefits you get back from that effort.

For example, the more effort you put into your fitness program, the more fitness you get back. But wait; it doesn't end there. The more effort you put into your fitness program, the more health you get back, the more energy you get back, the more stamina, the more strength, the more self-esteem, and the more "positive coincidences" you open yourself up to as well. "Positive coincidences" are the unexpected benefits that occur from effort. It's the things you can't predict that otherwise might not have happened unless you put in the effort. Einstein said, "Nothing happens until something moves." Well, once you get moving on your goals, through effort (focus, energy, and activity), you open yourself up to many positive happenings.

The more effort you put into your wealth program, the more wealth you get back. Wealth, which is not only money, but also includes money, is not a result of luck, but it is, rather, a result of effort. Effort is what opens the doorway to all of the good things in life, and anything of value, and, therefore, worth cultivating, requires effort. Relationships require effort. When people ask me about the secret to the success of my marriage, and why my wife and I are so happy together, I often wonder whether they are hoping I will say that I just got lucky. The truth is, the two of us have put in a whole lot of effort to make our marriage great, and guess what? It was worth the effort!

If you are reading this book, my guess is that you are someone who understands the importance of effort, and who is willing to put effort into things, especially, if it is efficient, meaning that it will, ultimately, pay off. Well, the first key to making any effort pay off is setting and working toward goals. *Efficient effort* is a concept I teach that involves performing consistent actions, while visualizing, in your mind, the specific goal you are working towards, simultaneously. To make your efforts efficient, it is critical to know what you want so you can formulate a plan to take you there, and that is what this goal setting workshop, and the strategies that follow, are intended to do.

Goal Setting Workshop

The goal setting workshop is divided into three stages. Each stage could be done independently, or they can all be done together. The stages correspond to what's going on in your life, right now, and to what you want to manifest for your future. For instance, in Stage One, we deal with improving what is going on, right now. There have been times in my life where I couldn't focus on the larger, future vision for my life because I was dealing with pressing immediate challenges. The solution was, to apply the skill you will be taught in Stage One. Also, in Stage One, we look at how to write out a vision for any goal, present or future, as well as how to generate ideas for its accomplishment. All in all, Stage One teaches the fundamentals.

Stage Two is the intermediate stage, if you can really call it that. Steven Covey, in his book *The 7 Habits of Highly Effective People* (a book I highly recommend), teaches us to "begin with the end in mind." In Stage Two you leverage this approach by imagining a time in the future when your life is exactly the way you want it, your future vision. From this future vision, you extract the various goals, which you can begin acting on, *now,* in order to manifest this vision.

Finally, in Stage Three, you simply identify all the various things you want to be, do, and have, listing them as well. This list is a living, growing embodiment of the interests and direction of your life, and it should be constantly expanding throughout your life. By taking the skills you learn in Stage One, and by applying them to every additional goal you determine, you will now have a template for focusing your mind and programming yourself for the inevitable achievement of your goals.

So let's begin. Set aside an hour, or more, of uninterrupted time. Grab several sheets of paper, or your Warrior of Life journal, and a pen, and get ready to begin with Stage One of our goal setting workshop.

Stage One

I can assume that, if you're are alive and reading this, there are things that are currently happening in your life. There are decisions and actions that you are taking, and there are decisions and actions that you are not taking (which is also something; don't be fooled, not deciding about something, is also a decision). The importance of this first stage is to help make sure that you are heading in the right direction: towards expansion, towards the positive, towards what you want, and away from what you don't want.

For the first step of this stage, begin by writing down all of the things in your life that you want to change. This could be a job or a relationship. This could be a behavior that no longer serves you; it could be a behavior, which you are not taking, which you'd like to do more of. This could be a circumstance or a situation that troubles you, such as poor health, low energy, or a job you hate. It could be a toxic relationship or something vague, like general procrastination. Don't write what you want yet, just write the thing you don't want. For instance, "Hate my job, no money in the bank, overweight, tired of being single, tired of worrying, servicing the old car cost too much, etc."

The first step to turning my own life around, was identifying all of the things I wanted to change. I no longer wanted to be bullied. I no longer wanted to feel afraid. I no longer wanted to be shy. Throughout my life, I still, constantly, analyze and reflect on what I am focusing on and how I am spending my time, to identify even more things I would like to change or improve. In the spirit of Kaizen, a Warrior of Life is committed to constant change and growth, "to becoming better today than yesterday" (one of the promises I made in the introduction that this book will help you to do). Through introspection and self-analysis, there will be things that come up, which we will want to change. Instead of complaining about them, as most people do, you will now have a formula for creating something new in their places.

The second step should be an obvious one. You're going to write down all of the things that you want instead. If you are not sure what you want instead, simply write down the opposite of everything you just wrote in the first step. Play with "inverse thinking," and write down, not only the opposite of what you don't want, but also the opposite of everything that you think you may be doing that is contributing to what you don't want.

For a simple example:

In step 1 you may have written, "I don't like my job."
In step 2 you would write, "New job."

In step 1 you may have written, "Don't want to smoke."
In step 2 you would write, "Perfect health and fitness."

The third step, which is one of the most important, is to take what you wrote in step two, and write a paragraph describing it, with as many descriptive words and adjectives as you can think of. This is where you create a basic vision of your goal. You want to be as descriptive as possible. You want to feel the positive feelings associated with the words you use to describe what you wrote in step two. This will serve as a recipe that you can refer to again and again to help you visualize your desires.

For instance, using the same example from before, you may write, "I have an exciting new job close to home where I'm working on fun projects, alongside a great team. The job I have is with a small company, which is growing and thriving. The people I work with are friendly and motivated, and they share similar interests. The job pays me a lot of money, and it offers a full benefits package. I am being positively recognized for my contribution, and I love going to work each day."

Don't skip any step. Each will be incorporated into the practices you will be learning in the next chapter, and, once you learn and apply those practices, they will aid you in accelerating your goal achievement.

The fourth step requires that you take several sheets of paper, using one for each goal. At the top of the page, write a summarized sentence for the goal. Each sentence should have the following characteristics: it must be positive, be present tense, be specific, be measurable, and have a target date. For example, "I now have a new job at a start-up software company paying $50,000 a year or more, with full benefits, within ten miles from my home, by March, 2012."

Underneath that summarized sentence, write down/copy the same descriptive summary you wrote in step three.

Then, for the fifth and final step, we invoke the power of "solution thinking". On the same page, begin listing as many possible solutions (often referred to as brain storming) to this challenge as you can think of. For instance, relating to our example about having a new job, you may list all the companies you know that you could work at, job boards you can put your resume on, recruiters you can talk to, people who you can network with, events you can attend, associations you can join, etc.

It is very important to leave room for more possible solutions and actions to be written down, as they come to mind. Do this for each of the goals you have summarized. Give each its own page. This list will be the framework for developing your plans.

Stage One Summary:

At this point, you have thought of and written down everything in your life you currently don't want. You then *substituted* its opposite in written form. In the third step, you described its opposite, the thing you want, in detail, using descriptive words that invoke emotion. After that, you summarized the thing you want (the goal) into a positive, present tense, specific, measurable sentence with a target date, for its achievement. For the final step, you then wrote a list of possible solutions, many of which are in the form of actions you can take. Using what you have learned so far about *Kaizen* and *momentum*, begin at once acting on the possible solutions you have written. If you wrote "post your resume on a job board," and you don't have a resume, make writing a resume an action step, and then do something immediately to help yourself gain momentum.

This is the formula for setting and achieving your goals; however, we are not finished yet. We have only looked at changing specific circumstances in your life. This is important, and very motivating, but it is only a third of the workshop. Now, we are going to focus on the larger picture of your life. We are going to create a vision of your future.

Note: Do the Goal setting workshop; don't just read this for entertainment. Every step has been developed, from years of trial and error.

Each step is important. For example, before I learned to apply step five, I used to just focus on my vision, taking too few actions. However, when I discovered the power of listing my vision, with my specific goal and its deadline at the top of a page, and then underneath it, "brain storming" every possible solution, my life began to change rapidly. My plans went from three possible options, to forty and fifty possible solutions. Within a short time, I had more opportunities than I could handle. I picked the best ones. Refer to the fifth step often, your solution list, and keep adding new possible actions. Then act! Do something, anything. Even the smallest step can help you gain the momentum you need; the smallest step can make the biggest difference. This isn't a cliché. You never know from your vantage point what one single action can do, so take the actions. A Warrior of Life is action-oriented, just as all successful people are.

Stage Two

Intentionally, some of the goals you just set in Stage One will make up part of the expanded vision of your future; however, you may find, as you do this, that the goals you just set are too small, and you need to expand them, as well. That is another intended purpose of this part of the workshop. Michelangelo said, "The greatest danger for most of us is not that our aim is too high, and we miss it, but that it's too low, and we reach it."

Creating a vision for your future will help you really to focus on what you'd like to create with your life. If you find you set some of your goals too low, that is okay; expand them.

To do this next exercise, creating a vision for the future, imagine that three to five years have passed, and you have manifested everything you could want in your life. What does your life look like? What are you doing? Where are you doing it? How do you behave? What do you have? Who have you become?

Typically, your vision will be a page or two, and it should include the key areas of life, such as health, family, work, contribution, lifestyle and growth.

Once you complete this exercise, you are ready to move onto the final stage.

Stage Three

Now, we are going to put to paper, in a cohesive format, all of the various things you would like to add to your life in order to enhance it and fully to express yourself.

Take three sheets of paper, and write this at the top of the first piece: What do I want to be? On the second piece of paper write this: What do I want to do? Then on the third page write the following: What do I want to have?

Now, take the goals you set in stage one, and place them on the appropriate page, under the appropriate heading. Next, look at the vision for your future which you created in Stage Two, and you will see that it is really a list of goals, in a paragraph form. Identify the goals; take each, and put it on the appropriate page.

Finally, once you've done that, write as many additional things you can think of on each of the corresponding pages, for example, I want to have a mansion, be a millionaire, run a marathon, start a charitable foundation, visit the Himalayas, start a romantic relationship, get new living room furniture, buy a race car, vacation in Aruba, etc. Have fun with this, and don't limit yourself.

Since we've already discussed how manifesting the things that you desire takes effort, we are now going to organize all of the items you have written to determine which of these to begin to give our effort to.

Read each of the goals you have written, and write next to it how long you think it would take you to manifest it. Write the amount of time in years. For things that you can achieve in one year write the number 1, for three or five years write either 3 or 5 next to it, and for goals you think will take longer than 5 years, just write 7. Even if you think the goal will take twenty years, just write 7 next to it. The reason for this is that I have found, when studying the approach of successful people, they estimate too little time for goals that they think will take them one year, often finding they take three or four years. On the other hand, they estimate too much time for their long term goals thinking it might take them ten years of working to save a specific amount of money or to launch a company, and then they find that it only takes them five to seven years.

Put all of the 1 year goals together on their own page. Do this for the 3 year goals, 5 year goals, and long-term goals as well which are labeled 7. From each page, choose the two to three goals that are most important from the rest, for you to have in your life, and, then, list them all on one single page. This page should have between fifteen to twenty goals to work on as part of your Warrior of Life Program. It is important to have a good mix of long-term goals as well as short-term goals, for the long-term goals, although far off, keep pulling you forward.

Now perform steps three through five from Stage One of this goal setting workshop. Do it for each of the goals you've chosen. Write a summarized sentence of your goal at the top of the page. Underneath that sentence, write a paragraph describing your goal, rich with adjectives. Finally, list as many possible solutions you have or actions you can take, to manifest your goal.

One final suggestion, look for actions that will contribute to multiple goals at once, and focus on those. For example, taking a class, or getting an education is something that can positively impact your work, finance, skill, and "thing" goals all at once. That would be a priority to focus on implementing immediately. *Most important, gain momentum by doing something, this instant!*

Chapter Summary:

Listing your desires in the forms of goals, describing them in a brief vision statement; listing all their possible solutions and taking action in the direction of your goals, is not something you do once a year, perhaps on New Year's Day. This is something that you do continually. Each day you want to be reviewing your main goals and planning how you are going to achieve them. This is key. Successful people, people who regularly manifest their desires, do so because they keep them in the tops of their minds each and every day. They wake up thinking about their goals; they focus on them during the day; they make sure that their activities match up with their goals, and they go to bed thinking about them. Unfortunately, the average person spends their days focusing on their worries and their problems, instead of on their goals, and they spend their down-time distracting themselves, through TV or something similar, from focusing on their problems or their goals. Don't let this be you. Keep all your goals handy in your Warrior of Life journal, and, then, do the process regularly.

We've already learned how, through our thoughts, we engage our personal resources, as well as the Universe, in attracting, to ourselves, the opportunities to manifest our desires. The determining factor, as to how quick these manifestations will take place, will be based on how much attention you are giving to them with your mind. Now that you have a list of goals to work with, we are ready to move onto the next level where we will concentrate on the mental techniques that will strengthen your focus and, thereby, improve your ability to manifest your desires rapidly.

Action Steps:

1. Do the goal setting workshop.
2. Record your goals and plans in your journal.
3. Take action on your goals, immediately, in order to gain momentum.
4. Schedule time, each day, to read your goals, and think of different ways to manifest them.
5. For each of your goals, examine ways in which you can apply what you have learned so far, such as substitution, momentum, and kaizen.

Chapter 7

Warrior of Life Mind Training

-Blue Belt through Black Belt-

Blue Belt

In the martial arts, the Blue Belt is typically an intermediate rank. By this point, the adept has been training for a couple of years, and the disciplines he has been developing are starting to show up outside of the training hall. Whether it is through a higher level of commitment that is demonstrated, for example, by arriving for work earlier and staying later than his peers, or through more confidence that shows up, when he voices his ideas in meetings or speaks in front of his colleagues, nevertheless, by now the intrinsic benefits of continued martial arts training are, ideally, having a measurable effect on the student's behavior and conduct. If you commit yourself to applying the techniques contained in this book, the same transfer of disciplines, to all areas of life, will be true for you, as well.

In fact, by this point, you have learned and, perhaps, have begun to cultivate many of the mental resources that are required to play a higher game in life, through the teachings in this book. The next step in the Warrior of Life program is to introduce you to a method that you are intended to apply on a daily basis, to continually condition your mind for goal achievement, authentic living, and success. This method, which the Warrior of Life makes use of, is the power of installing a daily success ritual.

Daily Success Ritual

Imagine a large pitcher filled with dirty water and each day you, purposefully, pour in a little clean, clear water. Perhaps, just several drops are poured in each day. Nonetheless, over time, the pitcher will become completely clear. This principle is the same with your mind. By performing a daily ritual, similar to the following, eventually you will have replaced the "dirty water" (the *poor conditioning* demonstrated by negative thoughts, limiting thoughts, limiting beliefs, doubts, fears, and worries) with "clear water" (*success conditioning* in the form of positive thoughts, positive expectations, empowering beliefs, confidence, and faith). That is what a daily ritual does for you. If performed in the morning, as recommended, the daily ritual has the power to orient your day in a positive direction. Fill your mind with positive, empowering thoughts and expectations, which will surely effect the way your day and, therefore, how your life turns out.

A Warrior of Life, like any successful person, is willing to do the things that the unsuccessful people just aren't willing to do. Creating and performing a daily success ritual is one of those things, even though it only requires a small investment of time and pays huge dividends in results and achievement. In studying with and talking to successful individuals, I have found it to be uncanny how many of them perform some sort of daily success ritual. For example, this very successful woman I know, named Gloria, remarked one day, over coffee how she spends every single morning, for thirty minutes to an hour, meditating and communing with God, through acts of gratitude and prayer. Another gentleman I know, named Dick, who is currently in his eighties (one of my mentors, who I will be writing about later in this book), and who has amassed a personal multi-million dollar fortune as well as several successful companies, has shared with me, that he spends every single early morning in quiet meditation, reflecting on his goals, his businesses, his various projects, and his plans for the days and weeks ahead. He also spends many afternoons and evenings reading biographies and business books. In his eighties, even though he is already a multi-millionaire, he is still working on improving and succeeding.

The Daily Success Ritual is a mental conditioning method, which makes up a necessary part of the Warrior of Life's approach to living. Ideally, at least thirty minutes each morning should be allocated to performing this daily ritual. If your schedule doesn't allow this, you can do some of it in the morning, and other parts throughout the day. The important thing is that you do something in the morning, even if it is for only fifteen minutes, to condition yourself for success that day.

The following are the components that make up the Daily Success Ritual. Throughout this chapter, you will find suggestions on how to best combine these components, as well as how to make use of them in other parts of your life.

Meditation

The first component of the Warrior of Life's daily ritual is meditation. Using our garden analogy for the mind, meditation is how we cultivate the soil for optimal results. It is in the silence of our mind that positive thoughts and intuitive ideas are able to bloom. The meditation you learned in chapter four has been designed to flow naturally with the daily ritual. As discussed, the first part of the meditation is designed to relax the body and store energy; the next part is for actively quieting and focusing the mind; the third part is meant to relax fully in the meditative state, and then the final part is for visualizing and affirming your goals and/or praying. *The components that make up this final part of the meditation we are going to look at more deeply in this chapter.*

Visualization

Visualization is the next component in the Daily Success Ritual. Visualization is one of the most powerful tools we have been blessed with as humans. The ability to visualize our desires has a very powerful effect on the subconscious. Everything in the Universe is created twice, first in the mind and then in physical reality. Visualization is the picturing power of your mind, and, when it is engaged on a regular basis, through mini-visualizations, throughout the day, and while meditating, it allows you to imprint your desires on your subconscious mind. In doing so, you are able to calibrate your awareness to be on the constant lookout for opportunities to manifest your desire in real-time (physical reality). Also, you invoke the creative, attractive power of thoughts which connects you through time and space to that which you want.

How many times in your own life have you dwelled on something in your mind, either good or bad, only to find yourself living it out sometime in the future? If you are like most people, you can think of countless times this has occurred. Oftentimes, people will dismiss it as coincidence, or as something they had to consciously work on to see become real. Well, if you've done it before, you can do it purposefully again and again. Make the powers of coincidence and *efficient effort* work for you. That is what visualization, affirmation, and daily action is all about—choosing efficient actions to perform and aligning yourself with life's coincidences—being in the right place, at the right time, with the right people.

Two years before I ever gained admission to my first martial arts class, I was already visualizing myself learning and practicing the martial arts. The more I imagined it, the better I felt (this is key). One of the most powerful principles in life is the "feel good principle". This says that people do things in order to feel good, and when something feels good they seek to do more of it. In the chapter on health I will talk more about this principle and how to make it work for you. Similarly, when you imagine what you want and it feels good, this feeling has a very potent effect on your thoughts. Feeling is the elixir which gives thoughts their attractive power. In addition, if it feels good you will want to repeat it. When what you're imagining feels good, you repeat imagining it, thereby opening yourself up to more and more possibilities for its manifestation. One of the coincidences I enjoyed from my frequent visualization of practicing the martial arts was being at the festival, on the day the martial arts school, which I eventually first studied at, performed. The next coincidence was when the bully who had been harassing me put cream in my hair, inspiring my parents to enroll me in the martial arts, bringing to me the very thing I had been visualizing. After two years of visualizing practicing the martial arts, I was now doing it in real-time. Looking back on this experience, I realize now, I could have expedited the whole process, if I had known the steps of the goal setting workshop presented in the last chapter. Had I been writing and affirming the goal, as well as regularly brain storming a list of possible solutions and taking action on each of them, I might have been enrolled in a matter of weeks. For example, a few of the actions I could have taken, had I been focused on it, would have been to ask a friend of mine who studied martial arts to have his parents talk with mine. Next, I could have started a martial arts club at school, or I could have walked to the nearest martial arts school (it was 1.5 miles away) and bartered with the instructor. Now each of these may have not worked out to get me what I wanted, but who knows what other opportunities they may have presented? My parents might have responded to any of these and signed me up sooner, or another amazing coincidence could have happened.

In another example, back in September of 2004, I interviewed for a great job at a leading Public Relations firm in town. After learning about the company from research and meeting with the CEO in an interview, I really wanted the job. A few weeks later, they hadn't returned my calls. I figured they weren't interested in me, yet I was still interested in them. Because they were located in town, I found myself driving by their offices often, and, without fail, every time I drove by their office, even without intending to, I would imagine (visualize) working there. I would think about what they had told me already about the job, and I would imagine what working there would be like. I'd even replay the interview in my mind, over and over again. Then one day in April, without any prompting by me, an email arrived from their EVP, asking if I was still interested in the position. Seven months had passed, with no word, and out of the blue, an email like this arrived. I didn't let this coincidence go unnoticed. I knew I had been visualizing this, and I was pleased to see this result. Needless to say, I accepted the job, and it was everything I had imagined.

One last story on the power of visualization, and then we will explore "active visualization" and how to make use of it most effectively to manifest your desires. In November of 2001, I walked into a restaurant for lunch, unaware that my life would be forever changed. The daytime hostess who seated me at my table was the most beautiful woman I had ever seen. Something mysterious about her eyes had captured my attention, and, as I watched her from my table, it was as if I was caught in her "siren song." However, I didn't want to hit on the hostess at her job. This wasn't my style, so, instead, I would often stop in for lunch and attempt to make conversation to create familiarity. I foolishly let this go on for months without ever attempting to ask her out, for I was afraid I'd make her uncomfortable, or, worse, she would see my as the type of guy that hits on the staff, at restaurants. Then, in March, while I was on vacation in South Beach, eating at an outdoor restaurant facing the street, I started imagining that I had seen her drive by. I, literally, thought I had seen her in a car driving by (by the way it wasn't her). I, then, kept replaying the scene in my mind, imagining again and again that she had driven by. That's when I realized, I had been thinking (visualizing) about this girl very often and it was time to take action (I should have done something sooner). Well, upon immediately returning home, I went back to that restaurant and asked her out. We've been married for seven wonderful years.

Visualization is very powerful. Visualization increases confidence. Visualization broadens awareness to opportunities and, most importantly, spurs action. Countless books have been written about its power; however, most people don't make active use of it. As I have mentioned, they often visualize about things they don't want to happen. To apply visualization in your life, begin by performing it at the end of the meditation, which you have been taught in this book. Once you have relaxed your body, taken control of your mind, and enjoyed the meditative power of just sitting, finish the session, every time, by taking a few minutes to visualize, with feeling, your most dominant aspirations. See yourself in the visualization. Include every detail, the smell, the sights, the sounds, and, most importantly, the feeling. Really feel the joy of experiencing your desires. Then, after a few minutes, let it go and continue on with the next part, which is affirmation. You will be amazed, if you do this each day, the changes that occur in your life, the opportunities that appear, the coincidences you notice, and the results you realize.

Affirm Your Goals

We manifest our desires through our thoughts, words, and actions. Visualizing is a thought activity, and is another application of the fundamental principle of success which is "thoughts are things". Speaking words, as I've already discussed, to makes changes in our lives, is also very powerful. Distilled down to its essence, though, the major determinant of how your own life will turn out is based on two things; how you communicate with yourself, and how you communicate with others. In both cases the communication relies upon words.

Words are very powerful. According to the Bible, the Universe was created with the word (see John 1:1), and you create your universe with your words. I talked about the importance of words in chapter two. Now you are going to make active use of words to help create your life.

Affirmations are our magic words. To affirm means to make true. When you affirm, you are stating something as true for yourself. By saying it is true for yourself, you are, in effect, orienting your mind in the direction you wish to take your life. There are two powerful ways to make use of affirmations, and I am going to share both of them with you, here.

The first way is to say your affirmation like an incantation. To perform an incantation means to chant your affirmation with repetition. This is very powerful. This is equivalent to pouring clear water into that jug of dirty water, as in the earlier metaphor. Drip by drip, the repetition of your desires pervade your mind, opening up your awareness to the means to make them a reality. There is one caveat: only affirm the things you are willing to take action on. Jim Rohn has often said, "Affirmation without action is delusion."

For example, if you are affirming like I did, "I am enjoying completing my marathon run," make sure you are actually getting outside, each day, to do some training runs. In other words, don't affirm, "I am completing a marathon," and then never get off the couch. It is not going to work that way, no matter how many times you say it. Of course, say it enough and you just might feel compelled to go for a run, and that might be all it takes to get you on your way to the goal.

The second powerful way of using affirmations is to phrase them as a question. As part of our natural inborn software, our mind is designed to answer questions, solve challenges, and seek out solutions, if, and only if, we present it to our mind as a question or challenge. By phrasing your affirmation as a question, your mind goes to work to identify possible answers or solutions opening the way for you, so you can identify opportunities to act upon.

Choose either of these two methods for reciting your affirmations, and apply one of them at this point in your daily ritual.

Action

This is the part of the recipe for success that is often not addressed enough by self-transformation and self-growth books. Much has been written about the Law of Attraction and visualization to manifest goals; however, there is only one way to accurately predict whether or not you are going to manifest your desire. In fact, if you want to foresee your future, the means will be presented to you after a little build-up. *Drum roll please.* What is the key to foreseeing your future, to determining the likelihood that you will see your dreams come to pass, and the only way to be certain you are on target to actually manifesting your desires? Action!

As part of the Daily Success Ritual, ask yourself each day, what actions am I going to take today? At the end of each day, ask yourself, "What actions have I taken today towards my goals?" The answers to these two questions will let you know whether or not you will succeed.

If you go two weeks, taking actions every day, and, then, you miss a few days, your future achievement, in direct proportion to this, is going to be very hazy to predict. Yet, if you take small steps in the form of daily actions, towards your goals, every day, your success is all but guaranteed. Here is the key: take the actions until you achieve your goal. If an action isn't working, don't change goals; change your approach. Persistence is not a mythical quality possessed by only a few; it is the act of taking simple, albeit even small, actions, every day, until you reach the goal.

Summary:

Make meditation the basis for your *Daily Success Ritual*. At the end of your meditation, visualize and affirm your goals (as incantations through repetition, with feeling, or as questions). Then decide what actions you are going to take to manifest your desires.

Next, go through your day on the lookout for opportunities, while taking action.

Also, take mini-visualization breaks through out each day. Spend just a few minutes visualizing your goal. When you can't visualize, like when you're driving, instead, vocally affirm and re-affirm your goals, as if you are pouring clean clear drops of possibility into your consciousness.

Perform your daily ritual of meditation, visualization, affirmation, and choosing actions, each day, without fail.

Brown Belt

The martial arts are rich with personal growth and self-development strategies and tools. Most are straightforward and have been written and recorded, first, in scrolls, hundreds of years ago, and, today, in books, like this one. Others are intrinsic in the structure of the martial art, itself, and are meant to be discovered by the student, through reflection and analysis. Hidden in plain sight, within the rituals, the words used, and the formal practice, are guidelines for achieving success beyond the confines of the dojo (Japanese for training hall). For example, the word sensei, as previously mentioned, translates to mean "the one who has gone before." There is an important lesson, tied up in the meaning of this word. When learning a martial art, it is vital that you train under a knowledgeable sensei who, as the meaning indicates, should have already travelled down the path you are embarking on. In other areas of life and fields of study, this is equally important. If you are beginning a new business, the ideal person, to seek advice and counsel from, would be a person who has successfully launched and developed a business, similar to the one you are endeavoring to start. If you are working to achieve a specific financial goal, the ideal person to turn to, for financial advice, would be the one who has already achieved the goal you are after, perhaps, one who has started in the same place you currently stand. This would seem to make sense; yet, more often than not, most people turn to the person closest to them, who is typically at the same, or, perhaps, at a worse vantage point than they are, and they ask that person for advice, instead of seeking the person who has been down the path before, who has done what they want to do, and who can show the actual way.

The lesson at this level is on choosing an appropriate guide to show you the way towards your goals and desires. There are several ways to do this. The first is, to identify a coach or a mentor who will work with you to show you the way. The second is, to identify someone who has done what you want to do, to discover how they did it, and, finally, model their approach.

Mentors, Coaches, and Modeling; these are the three types of guides we are going to identify to employ to assist us in manifesting our desires.

Mentors and Coaches

In my own life, I have been blessed with many wonderful coaches and mentors. I have also enjoyed the privilege of being both a mentor and coach for other individuals. You may be wondering the difference between a mentor and a coach. A mentor is typically an advisor, someone who shares the lessons derived from his own experiences, in the hopes of helping his mentee to navigate the course effectively. A mentor typically shares his knowledge and experience, gratis, often, getting his reward in the personal satisfaction derived from helping a fellow human being, rather than in revenue. In fact, I have found the majority of successful individuals whom we encounter are, typically, more than willing to share their knowledge and experience with those sincerely desiring to learn. The benefit of a mentor is he has been where you want to go and can show you the way if you are willing to watch, listen and apply his teachings.

A coach, on the other hand, is not focused, primarily, on sharing the best of himself, but, rather, on bringing the best out of the person he is coaching. A coach helps you discover the power and resources contained inside of you. The coach's role is to challenge you, to push you, essentially, to encourage you to discover the gifts you possess, and to help you develop those gifts to their fullest potential. The motivation a coach provides is not necessarily through "rah rah" but rather from encouraging you to examine, why you want something, and what is driving you. Your internal motivation, the reason why you want something, is much more powerful than any type of external motivation. This is often called your "Why?"

A friend of mine named Dave is a very successful mortgage broker. One of the reasons for his success is his willingness to do whatever it takes, to continually grow and expand his business. He is committed to constant professional growth. Well, due to the real estate and banking crisis, which has been recently affecting this country and the economy, he has had to face some of the most difficult challenges in his career. To best overcome these challenges, he hired a business coach. He has relayed to me, that the biggest value that this person has brought him has been helping him to stay, continually, focused on doing the handful of core actions that will keep bringing him his goals. Every time he gets distracted by the challenges of the job, his coach helps him to break free from the distractions and to regain his focus. As a result, his business has continued to flourish in this difficult economic climate, and when market conditions change, as they always do, and become more favorable, he will be in a position to soar.

In the first two chapters, I introduced you to my concept of creating a vehicle to put you on the fast lane towards success. As you learned, a proper vehicle contains a mentor or a coach. These individuals can easily be found in a variety of ways. At your current job, your boss may be an obvious, and willing, choice for a mentor. Perhaps, at a trade organization for your industry, you may discover individuals who can provide you with the guidance you desire. On the internet, in the yellow pages, and through referrals, you can most likely identify all types of coaches who you can hire to help you achieve your goals, such as fitness coaches, financial coaches, business coaches, and relationship coaches. Considering that even the teachers have teachers, and that the best athletes, most talented musicians, and most successful professionals, in the world, all have coaches, enlisting the help of a mentor or coach is not a luxury, but it is, often, a necessity.

Currently, I am blessed with many wonderful mentors who, willingly, share their knowledge and experience with me, on a regular basis. One of the factors, which has helped me gain access to these individuals, and which encourages them to keep teaching me, is my willingness to ask. I constantly ask for advice from successful people. When I am dealing with a challenge, I will go to the people who are in a position to guide me, and I will ask for some mentoring advice; as a result, I get it.

Your assignment for this chapter is to identify someone whose experience you can leverage in your own life, and, then, visit with them for some mentoring. Offer to take them to lunch or meet for coffee. Be transparent. Most people are willing to help.

Role Modeling

In chapter three, I talked about the concept of Act as If; and, role modeling is a very simple and powerful tool that is in line with that concept. One of the fastest ways to achieve your goals is to identify a person who has done what you want to do and, then, simply to model their approach. If they are within reach, you can turn to them for coaching. If they aren't in reach, modeling them by learning how they achieved the goal is a viable approach.

Through news articles, the internet, biographies, and other resources, you can, pretty much, discover how any particular success was achieved. Find out the steps; then, leveraging what you have learned so far in this book, visualize yourself achieving the goal; identify the actions you can take; gain momentum by taking small daily consistent actions, and add some rocket fuel by leveraging the advice of coaches and mentors.

This section presents a great opportunity to discuss the power of reading biographies and self-growth books. As you know, my life was changed when I discovered the wealth of knowledge available in books, and when I began to read and apply their lessons in my life. Since then, I have come to realize that "all achievers are readers." Reading is one of the most powerful habits you can employ to completely transform and enhance your life. I am assuming that, since you are reading this book, you, too, realize the value of reading. The intention I have is to motivate you to make reading a daily part of your life. In chapter nine of this book I will be sharing the Warrior of Life's daily success habits, and one of those is reading. Discover your own role models and success strategies through the daily habit of reading. Everywhere you go, have a book in your possession. Use the substitution principle and replace mundane activities, such as watching mindless TV, with reading a book, for your success. One simple idea, found in a book, can completely change your life. If things are not going the way you would like, if you are struggling with health, financial, or relationship challenges, measure this against the number of success-oriented books you have been reading. Jim Rohn said, "skip a meal, but don't skip your reading." Typically, I recommend a half an hour of reading a day; however, if you are broke or out of work, it might be wise to spend several hours a night, reading. Lastly, let the world come to identify Warriors of Life by how they always have educational books with them.

Black Belt

Congratulations! You have made it to the rank of black belt in the Warrior of Life mental development program. Well, not quite. What separates a black belt from the rest is the willingness to consistently practice and improve the basics, over and over again, until they are second nature (kaizen). Learning the advanced techniques can only come, once the basics have been sufficiently mastered. Nevertheless, your progress up to this point is commendable. Most people who pick up a book that could have a positive impact on their life, never even read this far, and many of those, who do, don't apply what they learn. Keep in mind, just as you discovered in my personal biography in the first chapter, the pursuit of black belt is not for what you get, but for what you become. Use this knowledge to become all that you are capable of, and your rewards will be better than any I can bestow upon you.

Action Steps:

1. Commit to performing the Daily Success Ritual for thirty minutes every morning for 21 days (the length of time it takes to form a habit).
2. Each morning ask yourself, "What actions towards my goal am I going to take today?"
3. Each night ask yourself," What actions have I taken towards my goals?" If the answer is none, don't go to bed, until you complete them.
4. Record your progress in your journal.
5. Identify someone, whose experience you can leverage in your own life, and visit with that person for some mentoring.
6. Look at your goals, and, then, find people who have accomplished the goals you are looking to accomplish (whether it's to lose weight, start a business, or find a mate). Model their approach.
7. Hire a coach.

Chapter 8

Forging the Physical Body

When we think about the various warriors, throughout history as well as those depicted in movies, one thing that often comes to mind is the level of fitness these individuals demonstrate, both in their appearances and in their performances. In the movie "300," for example, the Spartan warriors depicted on the screen, with their bulging muscles, are indicative of the level of fitness and power we expect from such heroes. These examples are not just relegated to history or to fantasy; modern day warriors, from all walks of life, embody this same level of commitment to fitness, and as a Warrior of Life you must expect nothing less from yourself. Early in my life, I was fortunate to recognize in my role models the virtues of optimal health and fitness, and I decided to make them absolute imperatives for myself, as well. This commitment to health and fitness has never wavered for me, and, over the last fifteen years--the present-day length of my professional career--I have learned and applied everything of value that was available to continue improving my health, fitness, and performance.

When I was in my senior year of college, in addition to teaching the martial arts at my own school, which was part of the local YMCA, I was also employed as a personal trainer for World Gym™. As a personal trainer, my role consisted of working with clients, to develop and implement a nutrition and fitness plan, which would help them to achieve their overall fitness goals. In the majority of cases, I was able to teach and inspire my clients as they made continuous improvements in their health and fitness. There was this one client, moreover, whose off-handed remark actually has held a significant place in my memory, often acting as an additional motivator in my life. One evening, while reviewing her nutrition plan with her and trying to help her devise strategies to implement the plan in her life, she continually made excuses, why this or that wouldn't work for her and in her lifestyle. I was still too inexperienced to realize, at the time, that it wasn't the plan that was the problem; it was, actually, her motivation. Looking back, I realize I should have spent more time examining the reasons why she wanted to improve her health and fitness (her "whys?" to do it), and less time worrying about the plan. Had she had enough reasons to change (the motivation), the plans would have taken care of themselves. In any case, I kept talking with her about the changes she should be making, the substitutions that she needed to implement, when finally she remarked, "This is easy for you to do; you have a cushy job."

Interestingly, I've kept that comment in the back of my mind and reflected upon it many times in the last fifteen years, when I found myself eating the right foods and doing the right things, even while working in different environments, which could be considered anything but cushy. In my first professional role, where I would often work non-stop, twelve-hour days selling cars for a local car dealership, I took delight when another salesperson playfully referred to me as "Wheat Germ," due to the healthy snacks I would pack the night before and eat during the following day. A few years later, while in another professional role, in which I found myself travelling the country over 225 days a year, I still continued to eat in an extremely healthy manner and exercise regularly. Never, in those travels, did I succumb to the ease of eating high fat, high sodium, processed, fast food while on the road. My vision of health that I held for my future was, and still is, too important to risk on faulty food choices. In addition, I also always motivated myself to exercise each day, no matter what. As a result, I have run the bike path from Venice Beach, to Santa Monica Pier, and back, several times; hiked the backcountry in Salt Lake City; saw most of Cleveland on foot; swam up and down South Beach; bicycled all around

Mount Snow, Vermont; and much more. Plus, all of these aforementioned activities were all squeezed in during business trips. One time, in particular, I finished up meetings in Los Angeles early, and I headed straight for the beach. I changed into swim trunks in the car, and then wandered out on the sand. There I saw two older women sitting in beach chairs, chatting in the sun. I politely asked them to watch my wallet, car keys, and cell phone to which they agreed, and I then headed into the surf to swim. Because I have always maintained optimal health and fitness, I have been able to do these things; because I do these things, I get to enjoy great health and fitness.

Optimal health and fitness is an interesting concept, for, not only is it a worthy lifelong goal, but also, it is often required in order to achieve many of our other goals in an effective manner. The bigger the goals you have for the different areas of your life, the more energy you need. High levels of energy are a positive and natural byproduct of a commitment to cultivating optimum health and fitness, through nutrition and exercise, as well as through the other actions, which will be taught in this chapter.

In the martial arts, yoga, religion, and other spiritual traditions, the mind-body connection is fully accepted as fact. As such, these systems have developed around the concept that the stronger the mind, the stronger the body can thus be; the weaker the mind, the weaker the body will inevitably be. The reciprocal is obviously true, as well. The more you commit to strengthening the body, the stronger your mind will grow, as well. These disciplines are directly connected. Develop a body of steel, and you will enjoy a steel-trap mind. The two go hand-in-hand.

One more thing, with the strategies you are going to learn in this chapter, mixed in with the discipline, which you will continue to cultivate, and the effort, which this discipline spurs, there is no reason why you cannot enjoy a powerfully healthy body, and an equally powerful mind all the years of your life. Accept nothing less!

Develop a Vision

Regardless of where you are in your level of fitness, the starting place for improvement is always the same, and it is based on what we have learned so far in this book.

Begin by developing a vision for your health and fitness. What do you look like? What can you do? How do you feel? How well does your family respond to your improved health and fitness? How well do your co-workers react to your fitness success? How are you spending your days and weekends? What clothes are you wearing? What have you always wanted to do in regards to health and fitness, but never could, or haven't done in a long time? Run a marathon? Hike a mountain? Play sports with your kids? Why is it important for you to be in terrific health, enjoying boundless energy and high levels of fitness? Why is it important to your family? What do you want to look like and be able to do, as you age? What health challenges do you expect to avoid, by improving your diet and level of fitness? These are the types of questions you want to be asking yourself, so you can create a future vision that appears on the screen of your mind that is rich with vibrant colors and sounds, and that inspires strong positive feelings within you. The vision, as you have learned, is very important. You want to be able to constantly refer to this vision, frequently, throughout each day, so it is accepted by your subconscious mind. Eventually, if you stick to your disciplined action plan, you will be able to see this vision on the outside, simply by glancing at yourself in a mirror.

Once you have this vision, write a summary of it as you learned in the chapter on goal setting. Be as detailed as possible. Next write the goal, or series of fitness goals, that are contained in the vision, each in a present-tense, positive sentence, with an estimated deadline by which you expect to see the results. Next, list all of the possible actions you can begin taking, right away (this approach was presented in chapter six in the Goal Setting Workshop). Keep this list nearby, and, as you read further in this chapter, write down some additional actions you can take, based on what you learn.

Here is a suggested first action: identify all of the things you are doing that are not consistent with your new goals. What foods are you consuming that are currently in the fridge or cabinets? What activities are you engaged in that are in contradiction to your new goal? Next, invoke the *substitution principle* and decide all of the things that you can put into their places. If you are eating junk food, what can you substitute in its place? When could you substitute exercise for another, less productive activity?

Now, gain *momentum,* by taking action. Throw away all the junk food. Go out and buy its healthy replacements. Go for a walk. Designate a few pages in your Warrior of Life journal to record your fitness goals and actions. Keep a food diary. Tim Ferriss, in his bestselling book, *The Four Hour Body*, suggests taking a photo of every meal you eat and posting it online in a social media forum. See what effect this has on guiding your behavior.

The great thing about starting a healthy living plan, versus beginning any other self-improvement plan, is that you can start taking action, immediately, or, at the latest, with your next meal. For example, if you decide that you are going to start a financial plan, and that you are going to save ten percent of what you earn, invest ten percent, and give ten percent to charitable causes (which is a great plan), you can't really put it into action until your next check arrives. With your health plan, you can start this instant. Throw away the junk, take a sip of water, choose a salad instead of a cheeseburger, and you are on your way. Identify yourself as a healthy, fit person, and reinforce that identity with "like" actions (actions consistent with your new identity, such as eating healthy foods, exercising, avoiding junk food, and skipping most desserts).

Next, follow this up, by listing a series of *rules* for yourself to guide your future conduct. A few paragraphs from now, we will talk more about rules; however, if there are things you are doing that you know you shouldn't be doing, make a new rule to live by. Here's an easy rule: don't eat fried food at fast food restaurants. If you must have something quick, order a salad. Write your rules down in your journal, and review them until they are habitual.

Choose a Vehicle

Just like the Samurai warriors of Japan, or the Navaho Indians of the Plains, who traveled together into battle on horseback, the aim of this next step is to choose a formidable vehicle, to help you achieve your health and fitness goals. As we learned earlier, the components of an effective vehicle include identifying a coach and/or mentor and being sure to "ride along" with a team of like-minded individuals. At this point, you want to experience the various vehicles that are available and choose the one that best suits you. The following are just a few suggestions, taken from my own life experience. As I already mentioned, the martial arts presents an excellent vehicle for transforming the mind, body, and also the spirit. Group fitness classes and group yoga classes present an excellent opportunity to study with, and alongside, other like-minded individuals, committed to health. Here's a suggestion: If you decide to begin taking yoga lessons, fully immerse yourself into the practice. Hang out with other students, who share similar goals. Subscribe to yoga magazines like *The Yoga Journal.* Eat vegetarian or vegan for a month, and record your experiences, lessons, and results in your journal. Rent or purchase yoga instructional videos. Go on a Yoga retreat. Buy clothes, specifically, for yoga. This list is practically endless. Make your new activity inspire you to adopt positive new behaviors and to establish beneficial new rules for yourself.

In 2009, I decided to run my first marathon. Instead of going this alone and doing my training solo, I combined it with my charity and giving goals; I opted to run with Team and Training, which is part of the charitable organization The Leukemia and Lymphoma Society. To become a member, I agreed to participate in raising donations for the cause, using running a marathon as a catalyst to gain proceeds from generous donors. In return, "my vehicle," Team and Training, supplied me with a running mentor and a coach, inviting me to group training sessions where I met with other like-minded individuals. I read books like *Ultramarathon Man*, by Dean Karnazes, and subscribed to a running magazine. I made some adjustments to my diet and exercise routines, consistent with what I was learning in the books and from the group. I competed in 5 and 10K races on the weekends, and I joined a running club. As a result, not only did I complete that marathon, but I also learned a tremendous amount about running, nutrition, and exercise, establishing several new habits, which I still maintain. In addition, the relationships I built, with my mentor and the other runners, I still cherish and continue to cultivate.

Immersion

One final strategy that hasn't been formally introduced yet, but was just mentioned and is encouraged to be a part of your approach, to achieving every goal you set and to manifesting all your desires, is to fully immerse yourself in the subject pertaining to your goal. One way to do this is offered by Brian Tracy, the famous speaker and trainer, who teaches that anytime you set a goal, you must also set a learning goal to go along with it. For example, if you set a goal to earn a specific amount of money, set a goal to read ten books on finances and investing. If you set a goal to travel to a foreign country, also set a goal to learn that language. When you set a fitness or health goal, perhaps it would also be wise to set a goal to learn a specific sport or discipline, and, then, read ten books on the subject, hire a fitness trainer, or do something similar. You can take this another step further, by choosing to immerse yourself in the subject by subscribing to magazines related to it. For example, I have read and subscribed to *Black Belt Magazine, Men's Fitness, Running, Entrepreneur, Success, Inc., Fast Company,* and *Parachutist,* to name a few. A few more ways to immerse yourself might be these: to do your research by going to clinics and seminars, inviting experts to lunch, watching related DVD's and instructional programs, and listening to audio books. Do what you can to become fully immersed in your subject. This is key!

So as you can see, there are many things you can begin doing, right away, this instant, to move you in the direction of your goal. I understand that, sometimes, it can be overwhelming to the point that many people find themselves not taking any action. This is why gaining momentum is so important by taking that first step. Remember, the leverage is not in the size of that initial action, it is in just getting started and staying moving. That is the essence of Kaizen: taking consistent daily actions towards your goal. When I was recovering from the torn Achilles tendon, as I previously have written about, and had been given approval by my doctor to begin resuming physical activities, I began very slowly and methodically. I had a vision of the type of health I insisted upon for my body--a vision I was committed to achieving--but I didn't set any short term goals, at first. Instead, I applied the principle of Kaizen to do just a little bit more each day. Soon, new desires began to manifest in my mind, and, eventually, as I have already mentioned, I was running a marathon, and my leg was back to a hundred percent.

The principle of Kaizen reminds me of the myth of Milo of Croton. Milo began lifting a calf, every day, starting with its birth. Eventually, by the end of the story, he was able to lift a full grown bull. The lesson of course is to do a little bit each day; consistency is the key. A word of caution for your fitness and your life: Beware the killer couch. Our bodies were made for movement. Movement typically equals growth, and, as you already know, "If you are not growing, you are dying." Use the principles of Kaizen, substitution, and momentum to get yourself to do something, the minute you arrive home from work. When you walk in the door of your home, immediately change into the appropriate workout clothes. Even better, schedule your workout with a friend, to ensure you keep your commitment to him or her and to yourself, to get out and move. Remember, movement equals life.

Disclaimer: As a result of my continued study into health and nutrition practices that has spanned at least the last sixteen years including work as a personal trainer, martial arts instructor, Yoga instructor, and health seminar instructor, I believe I am more than equipped to share with you the following strategies to build your own warrior level of health and fitness beginning with nutrition. However, before you begin any nutrition or fitness program, it is essential that you consult with a licensed medical doctor.

Nutrition

The martial arts originated in India and Asia, and, as they were refined over the centuries into their current incarnation, the eating practices of the martial artists were also refined. Both in China and Japan, the martial arts masters are very particular about what they eat, because they realize that nutrition has an immediate effect on their energy levels and their performance. As a result, nutritional strategies have been developed and passed down, both orally and in books. I was first introduced to these teachings in my early teens, when I was exposed to them through various books on the martial arts. These teachings inspired me to commit myself to perfect nutrition for optimum health and performance, and I have been doing so ever since. Through further immersion, I have become even more purposeful in my nutrition practices, and I am going to share them with you as some basic suggestions, which you can consider, as you develop your own nutritional plan.

First and foremost, approach eating for health and energy, as a natural part of your lifestyle, and not as something temporary, like a diet. If you are in need of a diet to lose significant weight, my suggestion is to approach changing your eating habits in the spirit of Kaizen, which is small, consistent changes done daily. The failing with most diets is that they are not sustainable, and, as a result most, people will notice a drop in weight early on, only to gain that weight back, and more, when the diet hits a plateau, or they let it go.

I also recognize that most people know what they shouldn't be eating and only eat those foods as a quick fix for hunger and low energy, or as a compulsion for sugary foods. By implementing the suggestions throughout this book, this behavior can now be changed, for you will have a strategy, and the reason behind it, to help sustain your positive eating habits. This section assumes you've done the important work already of creating a vision for your health and setting exciting goals with deadlines to aim for, as well as listing your motivations, which are you "whys" to do it.

I am not going to go into detail regarding all of the science behind these strategies, such as definitions of fats, proteins, and carbohydrates (macronutrients). As you immerse yourself in this subject, you can seek out that information, on your own.

The first rule is, eat breakfast every morning. This is very important. There are a variety of benefits derived from eating breakfast each day. The proper breakfast ignites your metabolism and sets a positive and healthful tone for the day. In addition, studies seem always to show that, people who eat breakfast, typically, eat fewer calories throughout the day. Eating slightly fewer calories each day than you use is the key to sustainable and healthy weight loss. A slight calorie deficit, combined with eating primarily low calorie, dense, highly nutritious foods such as vegetables, leads to a lean and muscular, healthy body type. Since breakfast is following the longest break most people go without food each day, it is important to refuel with a sampling of all the macronutrients. A proper breakfast should include protein, and this can be in the form of any of the following: eggs, lean meats, nuts, beans, or yogurt, to name a few. I believe that breakfast should vary on a daily basis, meaning that you do not have to eat the same thing every day. I suggest to people that they tailor their breakfast towards their planned activities for that day. A healthy ratio for breakfast (as with lunch, and dinner) should always be more protein, an abundance of vegetables, and a limited amount of complex carbohydrates, topped off with a small amount of healthy fats, such as oils, avocado, or nuts. When I discuss complex carbohydrates I am referring to both wheat products, and grains (starches). An example of a healthy breakfast following this approach would be two scrambled eggs, several asparagus stalks, and a half-slice of rye toast, topped with almond butter. Another example might be this: two lean slices of turkey, a side of avocado and tomatoes, and a half-slice of dry whole wheat toast.

Limit complex carbohydrates in the form of wheat and grain products and sugar products throughout the day, except on days with excessive amounts of cardio-type exercises (this is called carb-loading and carb-cycling). This overall strategy of limiting carbs and sugars in your daily diet is the key to removing body fat and improving overall health and energy. The Western diet includes way too much sugar, to the point that most people have become chronically addicted to high sugar intake. Significantly cutting back your sugar, is the best way to immediately improve your health and energy.

If you follow the forthcoming exercise suggestions in this chapter, you won't ever need to carb-load; however, I do realize that there are people who will want to test themselves, by running marathons and performing other endurances events. To sustain energy for these activities and the training they require, you need more glycogen, which is the conversion of carbohydrates consisting of wheat and sugar, stored as energy. If you are planning on performing an endurance activity on a particular day, add more carbs to your breakfast, but still include plenty of protein and healthy fats. An example would be a bowl of steel cut oats (carbs) with walnuts (protein and oil/fats) added. Otherwise, limit your carbs, each day, which leads to the next suggestion and, perhaps, the most important.

Reduce your total sugar consumption, including the sugars found in fruit (fructose), and in milk and yogurt (lactose) to less than *30* grams per day. Since most sugars are found in wheat and grain products such as cereals, breads, pastries, granolas, and chips, for example, by following this strategy to the letter, you will most likely be required to reduce these wheat and grain products significantly, as well (If you have a difficult time letting go of these types of foodstuffs in your diet, use the principle of Kaizen, and advance slowly in the direction of your goal, by limiting your intake, slightly, each day).

I wrote about personal success rules in an earlier chapter, and I wanted to share one of my personal rules with regard to health and fitness, which has worked extremely well for me. Before I present the rule, please believe me, I am not fanatical about nutrition, just very committed. I do occasionally enjoy a sugar-laden dessert treat. Therefore, the rule that I have for myself is, "I have to earn desserts." In other words, dessert for me is exactly what I think it should be (not what Marie Calendar or Sara Lee thinks), a reward for good behavior, a treat to occasionally enjoy, which, when approached in this way, actually affirms your good behavior, rather than deterring it. This says to your subconscious that dessert is a sometime treat, not an everyday thing. Most people don't have this rule. They'll have donuts and pastries in the morning, potato chips with lunch, a candy bar in the afternoon, and ice cream before bed. When it comes to your nutrition, perhaps you'll adopt this rule for yourself, or create your own.

Another rule I live by is to "choose to enjoy things that are good for you." Apply the substitution principle with regard to your snacks; choose things that taste delicious and that you can enjoy. To use the substitution principle, completely eliminate unhealthy options and replace them with healthier choices. For example, in the morning between breakfast and lunch I may snack on a small cup of fresh fruit, or an apple or a pear. Yogurt is a healthy option for a snack, as well. In the afternoon, fresh celery dipped in almond or peanut butter is a great snack. Granola is okay, but be very careful, for most granolas are laden with too much sugar. Stick to the strategy of limiting complex carbs, and, perhaps, use a little granola to sweeten plain yogurt rather than eat it alone. Nuts are a healthy snack, to be eaten in moderation, during the day. Dried fruit can be eaten if fresh fruit isn't readily available. Just remember to keep sugar amounts below 30 grams, for the entire day. If you've been a junk food eater, substitute these healthy choices, instead. I am often fond of saying, "Yogurt is the ice cream for healthy people," and, "Dried fruit is the candy for healthy people."

Eat much more vegetables. Vegetables are very important for creating a healthy body. Vegetables are very alkaline and prevent inflammation. If you eat a diet that is very acidic, or if you regularly eat large meals, which requires the body to produce copious amounts of acid for digestion, you can develop various forms of inflammation. Increasing your consumption of alkaline-rich foods, such as vegetables, prevents the production of excess acids in your body. Vegetables are those low calorie, densely nutritious foods, I wrote about earlier. Most people don't get nearly enough vegetables in their diet. Vegetables, besides being very low in calories, are rich in vitamins and minerals, and are highly alkaline. Though vegetables can be just as popular to eat in the morning like with an omelet, most people get their vegetables at lunch and dinner (if at all). The best suggestions I ever got for nutrition were the following: eat a salad at lunch and dinner, and fill fifty to seventy percent of your plate with vegetables. Then, fill the rest of the plate with a protein source, and leave very little room for complex carbohydrates like rice or bread (by the way, another great strategy that I am hearing more and more about is to eat off of smaller plates). Healthy proteins to choose from are wild fish, grass-fed beef, organically raised chicken and turkey, and other, lesser consumed, but equally good meats such as lamb and buffalo. Certain vegetables are high in protein. Also, eggs and various nuts, as previously mentioned, are great sources of protein. Healthy carbohydrate choices include anything that is 100% whole wheat, along with brown rice, quinoa, potatoes (especially, sweet potatoes), and oats (it's worth repeating that even "good" carbohydrate choices should be the smallest portion on your plate). Remember, even if they are whole wheat, or deemed healthy, you still want to significantly reduce their role in your daily eating. Ideally, eat small amounts of these types of carbohydrates, such as brown rice or sweet potatoes, earlier in the day, such as for lunch, and not for dinner.

In addition to being very alkaline, vegetables promote a healthy digestive tract, and, since eighty to ninety percent of immunity is in the gastrointestinal tract, this is very important. One other suggestion is based on something I have been doing for several years, which has acted almost like a panacea for me seeming to solve many health issues such as dry skin, acne, and what was occasional inflammation in the joints. This suggestion is to drink a greens drink daily. Your greens drink can be a combination of vegetables, which are juiced fresh each morning, or a greens powder, which you simply add water to. Amazing Grass™ is a company that makes a delicious, and highly nutritious, greens powder that I add to a glass of water in the morning, especially, when I am on the road.

The next strategy is taken right from martial arts literature, and that is to only eat until seven tenths full. The major challenge with eating until you are adequately full, or, ideally, seven tenths full, is that you are relying on a signal from your stomach, which medical scientists tell us is delayed and arrives several minutes after you are essentially full (which is why people continue to eat, until well after their stomachs are full). So the key to making this strategy work for you is to decide in advance, based on personal history and experience, what constitutes seven tenths full; then, use your discipline to control your intake. Also, fully masticate your food. The starting point of digestion begins in the mouth, where saliva works in tandem with the mashing power of your teeth to break down the food, and to help the body extract its nutrients. To do this, it is essential that you chew your food, until it is turned into a paste. In Buddhism, there is a practice called mindfulness, which teaches the practitioner to be fully present in their daily activities. Wherever you are, be there. Apply this to your life; it is what I like to call "mindful eating". Sit there and, really, enjoy your food. Begin by placing your fork down in between every bite. Don't keep shoveling food into your mouth. Instead, eat each bite, very slowly taking in the taste and the texture, noticing the ingredients, and enjoying every morsel. This, alone, will have a tremendous effect on your health and digestion, and, typically, it will cause you to eat less. Start this practice now. Key!

Another action is to plan all of your meals in advance. This has been a major factor contributing to the success of my healthy nutrition. I plan my meals, for the week ahead, the weekend before. I prepare my meals in advance, and, if I am going to be on the road and away from home, I pack a healthy meal and snacks in an insulated lunch box, to keep with me. This is a habit shared by almost all the health-conscious people I know.

Eat five to six times per day. Ideally, aim for the same portion and calorie sizes for breakfast, lunch, and dinner. Don't trust the old adage to eat breakfast like a king, lunch like a prince, and dinner like a pauper. A large meal, at any time of day, produces an exorbitant amount of digestive acid in your body, saps energy, fouls up your metabolism, and, typically, converts excess calories to fat. Instead, divide calories equally among the three main meals, and, if hungry, supplement a healthy snack, in between. For example, if on a 2,000 calorie diet, aim for 500-600 calories, maximally, each for breakfast, lunch, and dinner; then, limit yourself to 200-400 calories for snacks. With the advent of smart phones, there are currently a variety of free applications that will track, and measure, caloric intake for you, on a daily basis. I highly recommend My Fitness Pal. It is free; its library is very robust and contains many different foods and brands; it is also easy to use. It may be a real eye-opener for you when you come to realize that you are only eating 200 calories at breakfast, then 800 calories at lunch, thanks to the salad dressing and whole grain bread, and 1400 calories at dinner. Plus, the seemingly healthy fruit and yogurt parfait you picked up, actually contains 600 calories.

Some final suggestions, which have helped me in my nutrition, that may be helpful for you, as well, are these. Throw away the junk. Give it up. Stop drinking soft drinks; stop eating donuts; stay away from fast foods; put down the chips; avoid the pastries. Set rules for yourself that are indicative of the type of person you are becoming. For example, my wife and I eat pizza, but we refuse to eat a lousy "thirty minutes or less" pizza. We have a handful of pizza restaurants that we will go to, and we refuse to eat pizza, if it is not from these restaurants. As a result, we don't succumb to pizza in the office or at the mall, and we only eat it rarely, always at the best places. Before we go there, we earn it, with a quality workout. In addition, mindful eating during the meal ensures that we enjoy every morsel. Personal success rules-earning it- mindfulness; putting these strategies together is how this stuff works best! So, yes, we are pizza snobs, as well as pastry snobs. We don't eat dessert, unless it's the best option. Whereas most people eat dessert every day, and it's mundane ninety-nine cents stuff, like a morning donut, an ice cream cone, or buttered popcorn, we may only eat dessert once every two weeks, but, when we do, it's decadent and we share. Be consistent with the good stuff and very inconsistent, with the not so good stuff.

In addition, replace all beverages with water, vegetable juice, or tea. Except for one small cup of coffee each day, and the occasional glass of red wine, with dinner, I primarily drink water. All my research tells me that the average person should drink half their weight in ounces of water each, and every, day (fire up your metabolism by putting fresh lemon in your water). Most people go through life dehydrated, and, as a result, toxins build up in their bodies. On the other hand, by combining drinking copious amounts of water with eating vegetables, which are essentially water-rich foods packed with vitamins and minerals, we can provide our bodies the means to eliminate toxins. Make drinking half your weight in ounces of water a daily action. Write it down, and begin it now.

These are just some suggestions to get you started on your nutrition plan. Immerse yourself in the subject, and begin making changes in your own life. Also, share these strategies with the people you care about. Hold yourself to a higher standard, and put your reputation on the line, both by being vocal about and by being a physical example of, healthy living.

Exercise

Exercise is not a luxury; it is a necessity. As I've written throughout this book, our bodies were made for movement. Through exercise we help eliminate toxins, strengthen muscles and bones, remove dead tissue and cells, strengthen our organs, improve cardiovascular health and blood flow, improve digestion, and gain many more benefits. The challenge is that the modern conveniences of life have left most people sedentary, and, as a result, they have been missing out on the benefits, just mentioned.

Lack of exercise leads to deterioration and disease. This is a fact. Moderate exercise, performed daily, is a natural way to sustain health; increase energy and vitality; and enhance the ability to perform at work, in recreation, and romantically (wink wink).

What follows are some suggestions to making exercise a natural part of your lifestyle. These are just some strategies I have learned along the way. They are not meant to be a be-all-end-all, by any means; in fact, if you have health and fitness goals and are using the goal setting and achieving process presented in this book, your action plan will include learning more about exercise, from a variety of sources.

Here are some musts. Everyone must do some sort of strength training, at least two to three times per week. Strength training puts healthy pressure on the muscles and bones, forcing them to adapt and grow stronger. Stronger bones are valuable throughout life, but they appear even more so, when you are in your later years. Strength training also exercises the heart and nervous system. Strength training is typically done by lifting weights. Going to a gym, or lifting weights at home, a few times a week, is crucial for everyone. Common alternatives would be to lift heavy things like rocks and furniture, or trees and tools. Those are good too. I'm just suggesting that, for most people, lifting weights is one of the more efficient ways to strength train. If you are not lifting heavy things, you are missing out on a crucial ingredient for a healthy life. People who exercise daily, but only do cardiovascular exercise, such as running or cycling, without combining strength training, may be doing more harm than good. Our bodies adapt to resistance and will look for the easiest (most efficient) ways to fuel themselves, and, without a demand for the type of strong muscles, which strength training develops, the body may eventually cannibalize itself in the process. Don't believe me? Take a look, the next time you see chronic, long distance runners going through your neighborhood. Their legs are typically thin and "bird-like," compared to those who strength-train.

As a part of my own strength training regimen, I typically lift weights three times a week. During these times, I perform a variety of basic exercises with heavy weight, for six to ten repetitions, per set. The exercises I do combine barbells and dumbbells, and they consist of various squats, bench presses, military presses, deadlifts, and rowing exercises. I choose exercises that combine multiple muscles in one movement, versus targeting a specific muscle. The sessions typically last no more that forty-five minutes, and they are followed by a cardiovascular activity.

Cardiovascular exercise, which refers to exercises that increases heart rate and respiration (breathing) for a specific period of time, should be performed three to five times per week, for a minimum of twenty minutes, to a maximum of forty minutes. This advice may seem contrarian to my own behavior, since I have mentioned competing in endurance events, such as running a full marathon; however, these experiences have shown me the value and importance of limiting cardiovascular output sessions to forty minutes, maximum (ideally thirty minutes), versus four hours, or even just one hour, for that matter. Options for cardio include running, swimming, biking, spinning, hiking, aerobics classes like Zumba, or even walking at a brisk pace, to name a few. Cardio exercises performed for longer than forty minutes can become catabolic, meaning that your body uses muscle as an energy source. Cardio types of exercise are great for the cardiovascular system, hence the name, and are also extremely valuable for the brain. Science has shown measurable improvements in brain function, due to cardio exercises like running. Starting your day with a thirty minute run is a great way to leverage this benefit, and you can make it part of your "daily success habits"(see chapter nine).

Flexibility training, such as stretching before and after workouts, as well as several times throughout the week, is important for overall fitness and for preventing injuries. It is also important for healthy energy flow through the body. I typically combine stretching with my strength training and cardio routines, as well as take classes in martial arts and yoga, which put a heavy emphasis on flexibility. However, simply choosing to sit on the floor of my living room and stretch, while watching a television program, works, as well.

There you have the three main components of holistic exercise: strength training, such as lifting weights; cardiovascular exercise, such as running; and, also, stretching. What I have found to be one of the most powerful ways to combine strength training, cardiovascular exercise, deep breathing, and flexibility into one effective workout, which can be, pretty much, performed anywhere, is by performing exercises using one's own bodyweight. Bodyweight exercises, such as those I am suggesting, are very prevalent in the martial arts. These range from simple exercises, such as a push-ups, pull-ups, squats, and planks, to more complex exercises, such as handstand push-ups, backbend push-ups, one-legged squats, and hanging leg raises. Bodyweight exercises, such as those taught by fitness expert Matt Furey in his bestselling book, *Combat Conditioning*, which combine multiple movements into each exercise, such as in the Hindu push-up and the Hindu-squat, are even more holistically beneficial. These types of exercises are ideal for increasing energy, strength, stamina, and overall fitness. Bruce Lee is often quoted as saying, that the best exercises are those, which require mastering your own bodyweight. Performing a twenty minute routine of bodyweight exercises is enough to thoroughly challenge the muscles, and exhaust the body of toxins. For more information, I recommend checking out Matt's book, *Combat Conditioning*, which can be ordered off his website http://www.mattfurey.com

When am traveling a lot, and my schedule doesn't allow me to get to a gym, I will often do a twenty minute run around the hotel area, and, then, finish up with fifteen to twenty minutes of bodyweight exercises, typically Matt's stuff. This can also be worked into your weekly routine, at home. Perhaps, on Monday and Wednesday, you lift weights in the gym, while combining bodyweight exercises into your routine. Sunday, you bike with friends. Tuesday and Thursday, you take yoga. Friday, you perform a bodyweight routine at home, and, Saturday, you run or hike through the woods.

Similar to bodyweight exercises, as just described, is the practice of yoga. Yoga can be performed statically, by holding various postures (asanas) for a minute or two, or actively, as in the case of a vinyasa, in which you perform a series of postures, one after the other. Both practices are very effective for improving strength and cardiovascular health. Yoga is great for strengthening and stretching muscles, improving joint flexibility and joint health, calming the mind and body through deep breathing, and burning calories, through the intense muscular strength required to hold an asana, or perform a vinyasa.

One final suggestion: have fun with your routine. Be like a child, and play. Exercise with your friends. Have friendly competitions. Run 5 or 10K road races on the weekend. Most of all, make the exercise enjoyable and fun. Also, exercise in brief periods throughout the day. When I am working in an office, my colleagues are no longer surprised, when they walk by my office and see me on the floor, in my dress clothes, performing the Hindu push-ups I learned in Matt's book Combat Conditioning. Exercise regardless of location. Do push-ups or squats while waiting for a bus. Do sit-ups or planks during commercials, while watching TV. Do pull-ups at the park, when you take your kids out to play. Take the stairs instead of the elevator. Make movement a central part of each and every day.

Action Steps:

1. Create a vision for your health and fitness.
2. Write a list of goals, consistent with your vision. Be specific, make sure the goals are measurable, and include dates for their achievement.
3. Choose the most pressing goal, to begin working on immediately.
4. *Take an action right now, to gain momentum.*
5. Identify what is currently in your life, which is contrary to your goal. What habits do you need to change? What foods can you throw out of the kitchen? Do something new.
6. Enlist a friend to exercise with. Schedule the time.
7. Keep track of your progress in your journal.
8. Drink plenty of water throughout the day.
9. Purchase a book like Combat Conditioning and begin doing the exercises.
10. Sign up a for a 5k run/walk event.

Chapter 9

Ultimate Life Success

Life Mastery is at the core of what this book is about, and to become a master, you must do what the masters do. The masters realize the vital importance of taking the time, each day, to invest in themselves and their own growth. You've learned so far, how the philosophy of Kaizen can be applied to accomplishing a goal, or to improving a particular area of your life. Well, Kaizen has a much broader purpose, as well. By putting the right system in place, you can dramatically transform and improve every facet of your life. If you simply make small investments of time to nourish yourself, throughout each day, this practice compounded annually is guaranteed to produce massive results. The following daily success habits are based on my own experiences studying with the masters in various fields. Individuals who are masters of money, business, relationships, sports, and life apply these practices in some fashion, almost every single day. You will notice that the first three habits are part of the Warrior of Life "daily success ritual" which you learned in chapter seven. Do this every morning to orient and focus your day. If your morning schedule allows, take some of the other daily success habits and make them a part of your morning "daily success ritual," as well. The key is to do this every single day. The rewards will be worth it. Also, you can practice these first three habits again, at various times each day, to increase their effectiveness.

Daily Success Habits

1. Meditation. The benefits of meditation have already been discussed, and they include improving focus and cognition, lowering blood pressure, reducing stress, and enhancing peace of mind. The "daily ritual" combines meditation, with visualization and affirmations, in one, thirty minute session at the beginning of the day. It is highly recommended. Do this for thirty days, and you will never want to stop.

2. Visualization. First, be sure to perform the "daily ritual" each day, which includes visualization. In addition, ideally, take time throughout the day to visualize yourself enjoying the achievement of your goals and desires, and living out your dreams. Also, take the time to visualize yourself performing well before any event, whether it's conducting a sales presentation or giving a speech. Each visualization session should take no more than five minutes, and it should combine as many details as possible.

3. Affirmation. Affirmation and positive self-talk go hand in hand. Throughout the day, repeat affirmations of your goals, as well as positive statements, to control your focus. Some additional ones to consider are:

- Every day, in every way, I am getting better and better.
- I can do it.
- I am healthy, wealthy, and wise.
- Why do I always perform so well?

Use positive self-talk to influence your behavior as well. Get yourself to take the actions you need to take, by inciting yourself to action, through affirmation. The late W. Clement Stone, the founder of the insurance giant, Combined Insurance and the publisher of *Success Unlimited,* is known for having his employees affirm, each day, as an incantation, the phrase, "I do it now. I do it now. I do it now." This is a great incantation to do to overcome procrastination. In fact, this is also the same affirmation Stone himself would say early in his career, when he was experiencing

146

doubts and fears about taking an action that he knew he must take, such as calling on a large prospective client.

4. Journaling. Take time throughout the day to write and re-write your goals. Capture good ideas in your journal. Solve problems by thinking on paper. Turn the problem or challenge into a question, and list twenty possible solutions. I have found my personal journals to be the most efficient place to keep all of my goals, plans, and strategies. They are also the best place to work out challenges on paper, capture great ideas, and record inspiring quotes and lessons. Make your journal a representation of your commitment to living a life of success.

5. Read. Readers are leaders. Every successful individual I know is a consumer of great books. One of my mentors is eighty-one years old, and he is still reading personal development books, such as books on improving his health, relationships, business and life. Spend at least thirty minutes, each day, reading. It is better to miss a meal in a day than to miss your reading time. You can become an expert in your field by reading related books. Expand your horizons by reading books about other industries and fields, as well. A common business practice, performed in a different industry, might completely revolutionize your company, if you were to discover it and apply it in your field.

6. Exercise. Exercise has a positive impact on the body and the mind. Study after study shows people who exercise enjoy increased brain function. Cardio exercise, in particular, has a positive effect on the brain. The body and brain are made for, and respond to, movement. For the best effects, perform cardio exercise in the morning, such as running, walking, or an intense bodyweight routine. Perform strength training, such as lifting weights, yoga, calisthenics, or martial arts in the evening.

7. Thinking time. Make time for thinking about your life, each and every day. Analyze what's working and what's not working. What actions should you be taking and which should you stop taking? Take thirty minutes a day where you sit with a notebook, or your journal, and focus on generating ideas. Do it in one session, or break it up throughout the day. For example, take fifteen minutes in

the morning, to plan the day, and fifteen minutes in the evening, to reflect on the day. Take thirty minutes on Sunday evening, to plan your week. In addition, use this time to reflect and to analyze what's going on in your life, your relationships, and your work. Leverage what you learned in chapter three on introspection, and apply it each day during your thinking time.

8. Eat nutritiously, and drink plenty of water. Plan your meals with the same care that you would plan anything important in your life. Food is part of the building blocks of life, and the food you eat affects your health and your energy, which translates into your ability to achieve your goals. (Refer to the previous chapter for more information on nutrition and exercise)

9. Practice Gratitude. In the morning, evening, and throughout the day, make sure you are taking the time to be grateful for all of the blessings in your life. This includes the people, the things, and the opportunities you enjoy. Typically, in the mornings, when I am driving to the office, I will say out loud all of the things I am grateful for in my life. I usually pause after each one, and take a moment to let the feeling of gratitude for the particular blessing, resonate through my entire body. I, also, focus on my blessings when exercising. What better time to appreciate the gifts of health and fitness than when you are experiencing them in your life?

Track Your Habits

What gets measured, gets done. By tracking your progress, each day, you are practically guaranteeing the adoption of these habits, in your life. Here are two approaches that have worked exceedingly well for incorporating these habits into a person's life.

When I first began discovering these practices, and decided I wanted to incorporate them into my own life, I would take a 3x5 card, and, on one side, I would write my top three goals, to read throughout the day. On the other side, I would write the above, daily success habits, like a checklist. As I went through the day, I would frequently refer to my checklist and perform the aforementioned activities. When I completed one, I would put a check next to it. I would then repeat this practice, the very next day. Eventually, these all became a part of my daily lifestyle and no longer required the checklist. I still write my goals on a 3x5 card and keep it in my pocket to read throughout the day.

Another approach I like was created by one of my students, who designed a spreadsheet that he keeps on his computer. In the left column of the spreadsheet, are the nine habits, and then to the right, are each of the days of the week. He then keeps track, on a daily, and weekly, basis, how well he is tending to these basic habits for success, by checking them on his spreadsheet. Find what works best for you.

One more suggestion: *What gets scheduled, gets done.* Grab your weekly planner, and block out time, each day, for these activities. Including exercise, cumulatively, the nine habits, you just read about, add up to a small part of your day. Set aside one hour, maximum, in the morning, for the daily ritual and reading; thirty minutes, before lunch, for thinking time; one hour and fifteen minutes, for exercise in the afternoon; and a half hour, to work in the rest. Gratitude and affirmation are activities which can take less than a minute and can be performed while doing other things in your day.

By practicing these habits, each day, you are building your mental and physical reserves, which are crucial for being able to take advantage of the final, two life success strategies in this book.

The following two strategies (one in this chapter and one in the next) are what identifies the Warrior of Life, and separates him or her from the pack. Often misunderstood, these two approaches practically guarantee more success, in all areas of life. Unfortunately, most people run in the opposite direction of what you are going to learn, next, in this chapter. For this reason, they live lives of mediocrity, never knowing for themselves what Roosevelt meant when he said, "The credit (rewards) belongs to the man who is actually in the arena, whose face is marred by dust and sweat and blood, who strives valiantly, who errs and comes up short again and again, because there is no effort without error or shortcoming, but who knows the great enthusiasms, the great devotions, who spends himself for a worthy cause; who, at the best, knows, in the end, the triumph of high achievement, and who, at the worst, if he fails, at least he fails while daring greatly, so that his place shall never be with those cold and timid souls who knew neither victory nor defeat."

Persistence

Before we go into these final strategies, we must examine the thread that holds all of this together, which is persistence. Persistence is the ability to stick with a goal until it is achieved. Persistence means never giving up; it requires the willingness to go over, under, around, or through any obstacle that stands in your way. The ability to persist comes from within, and, as such, it can only be cultivated within. Persistence is a quality, typically associated with a strong mind, body, and spirit. Thus, to strengthen your resolve to persist, you must work on the inside, by visualizing your goals several times, each and every day. By continually focusing in your mind's eye on your goal, you develop the type of clarity that invokes all of your senses. The goal becomes so attractive, that your mind and emotions are fully engaged. With clarity, you come to that place, where your desire is something that you want to manifest with all your heart, body, and soul. In addition to visualization, solution thinking is another powerful method to strengthen your resolve. When you focus on solutions, you become internally motivated to actualize those solutions in reality. Positive self-talk, in the form of affirmations, repeated daily, also helps engage your subconscious mind, to fuel your ability to persist. Surrounding yourself with like-minded achievers, is yet another way to practically guarantee your willingness to press on in the face of adversities.

Note: The previous paragraph presented a summary of some of the various concepts you have learned, so far, in this book. They all work, that is, if you are willing to work them. My suggestion is to read, and re-read, this book. I've removed a lot of the fluff, making it as specific as possible. As you read, identify how you can make these strategies a part of your life, and take action immediately.

One of my personal mentors is Dick Minervino. I met Dick when I was hired to help launch one of his companies. Dick was born during the Great Depression, and he grew up feeling the full negative effects of the Depression. However, with only an eighth grade education and thirty-five hundred dollars in his pocket, he went on to create several multi-million dollar telecommunication companies. At this moment, he is an eighty-one year old fountain of energy. He works at his company five days a week, often putting in twelve hour days. He is currently in the process of building what may soon be the largest philanthropic foundation in history, designed to help individuals from all walks of life to save money for their futures, while learning the value of a dollar and the keys to fiscal responsibility. I have been fortunate to spend many hours alone with him, enjoying the benefit of his experiences and his philosophy for success. He continually inspires me to dream big goals and to take consistent action. He once summed up his strategy for success into one concise sentence for me, and, now, I am gladly sharing it with you. Dick said to me, "The key to success is to keep putting one foot in front of the other." That's it, in a nutshell. A simple, easy to understand clue on manifesting a life of success is summed up in the one enigmatic phrase, "keep putting one foot in front of the other."

The lesson: set a goal that inspires you and challenges you, and, then, persist to manifest it, no matter what the obstacles. When in your pursuit, when you are face to face with the most difficult times, or when you are enjoying advantageous times, you will guarantee your success through persistence. Putting one foot in front of the other.

The Ultimate Life Success Strategy

Setting audacious challenges or seeking them out is the ultimate success strategy. The greater the challenge, the greater, usually, is the reward. The reason most people don't enjoy much of the rewards available in life, is because they don't set large enough challenges for themselves. If your goal is just to get by, that is what you will get, and, in my experience, that is what most people are aiming for: just to make a living, or to just get through the day. However, if you dare yourself something mighty, and develop the skills and resources to achieve it, while persisting in the face of all obstacles that come your way, then to you all of life's rewards shall be given. I'm not talking about just material things, but other rewards, such as the self-esteem and personal satisfaction of seeing a challenge through to the end; the joy of being a role model for your children, and the happiness derived from living a life of substance.

The initial challenge I set to totally change my life, to improve myself, and to overcome all of my fears and weaknesses, while developing all of my strengths, seemed so ambitious to me at the time; nevertheless, I committed myself to earning a black belt, jumping out of planes, walking on fire, and traveling long distances to train with the masters; I read hundreds of books, and I sought out teachers, coaches, and mentors. I worked to achieve all of the goals that I then set for myself; however, just as the challenge was great, so, too, was my level of persistence. The greatest reward, from that challenge, was not the experiences themselves, though they were extremely valuable and life-changing; it was not the wonderful relationships I cultivated, or the piece of black cotton that was eventually adorned around my waist, oh no; the greatest reward was what this challenge made me. As Jim Rohn says, "The greatest value in life is not what you get; the greatest value in life is what you become."

In the previous chapters, I talked about my experience, running my first marathon. What I didn't mention is what inspired me to set this goal, which was tearing my Achilles tendon. Soon after I finished rehabilitation for my previously torn tendon, I realized I needed a new challenge, to affirm my health. I decided to complete a goal I had set many years before, one which I had placed on the "back-burner": to run a marathon. Even though, due to the injury, my recent exercise level had lowered, and the fear that I might re-injure myself was still looming, I knew I could accomplish this goal. I had the skills and resources gained from overcoming many other challenges and achieving similar goals, and this brings with it a key point: all disciplines transfer. Many skills transfer, as well. If you become successful in one area of life, you can position that success as a springboard to achievement, in other areas of life. I recognized that running the marathon was a mighty challenge, considering my current condition; however, being a Warrior of Life, I decided to make it even more compelling. In order to make completing the marathon a bigger challenge, I batched it with my charity and giving goals. I previously mentioned how I joined a wonderful organization called Team in Training, which promotes endurance events in order to raise money for the Leukemia and Lymphoma Society. After agreeing to raise several thousand dollars, I then reached out to all my friends and family, and I told them my commitment, asking them to donate money to the Leukemia and Lymphoma Society, in support of my efforts to run the marathon. To top it all off, I decided to complete all of this in only four months. When race day arrived, I had achieved my charitable giving goal, and, a few hours later, my goal of running a marathon was achieved. The good news was, I put myself out there, and both were a success. Even better, I had grown in many positive ways as a result.

Embrace Large Challenges

The fastest way to grow to the top of your field or company, in business, is to take on large challenges. Identify the biggest problems a company faces, and commit yourself to solving them. A financial truism is that money and responsibility go hand in hand. The more responsibility you take on, the more challenges you solve, the more money you typically receive. The CEO of Disney is responsible for a vast enterprise, spanning multiple theme parks, products, and entertainment media, including movies and TV shows, and he has responsibility for thousands of employees and shareholders; as a result, he earns one of the highest incomes in the world.

Lee Iacocca became famous in the 1970's when he took on the challenge of rescuing Chrysler. I was just a small child when this was happening, yet today, people still know his name, and he is widely respected in business. More recently, Lance Armstrong set the audacious goal of winning The Tour de France after surviving a battle with cancer, in which he had a twenty percent chance of surviving. Back then, would he have referred to that as simply a goal, or, perhaps, the greatest challenge of his life? Be no less committed to setting amazing challenges, for yourself, as well. Set the type of challenges that keep you up at night scheming, plotting and planning; the type of challenges that get you out of bed early in the morning and keep you motivated throughout the day; the type of challenges that force you to read the books, attend the classes to learn new skills and meet new people. Set the kind of challenges that will make something out of you, in order to achieve them.

Challenge and risk, typically, go hand in hand and should be welcomed. Often, the greater the risk, the greater is the reward. My brother Anthony is a great example of a professional risk-taker. After finishing college, he went to work for the United States Senator, Chris Dodd. Starting out at the bottom of Dodd's staff, he earned barely $20,000 a year. To maintain his lifestyle, he had to work a second job, and he had to plot and plan his moves carefully. For the next seven years, he tirelessly worked his way to the top of Dodd's staff. To do this, he would often work seven days a week, sometimes twenty hours a day. Eventually, he was Dodd's Community Affairs Director, his driver, his body man, and many other roles as well. After seven years with Dodd, he saw an opportunity to make a real difference, lobbying for the good guys, while working at a large and successful firm. However, everyone he asked for counsel suggested that he stay with Dodd; stay in that side of the political arena; making the move was very risky to his career and his future. He took on the risk anyway. For several years, he grew as a lobbyist and found himself earning a sizeable income, with security and great prospects for the future. As a lobbyist, when the legislature was in session, he would be putting in twenty hour days. How many people are willing to do this? That he flourished is indicative of his commitment to his clients, and of his willingness to put in the effort to get what he wants, regardless of how demanding the requirements. People took notice of his work ethic, which is why it was no surprise to me what happened, when an opportunity presented itself for him to join a colleague and launch their own firm. This would be a huge challenge with a lot of risk. His current employer would stymie any attempt to keep his own current clients. They'd be starting from scratch and giving up the secure pay and benefits they enjoyed. Again his friends and family suggested he stay put (well not all of them, wink, wink). He didn't listen and launched his firm. Currently, he earns well over ten times the income he first made, is respected in his field, and is making a measurable difference in his home state, and beyond. What has helped him enjoy a constant trajectory of upward business success? The answers are his willingness to set and pursue worthy challenges, and his commitment to putting in as much effort as is required, and then some more.

Leo Buscaglia is quoted as saying, "The person who risks nothing, does nothing, has nothing, and becomes nothing. He may avoid suffering and sorrow, but he simply cannot learn and feel and change and grow and love and live." I couldn't say it better myself. Better to dare mighty things!

If you have time to come home each and every night and relax in front of the TV, if your work is stagnant; if you are overweight, in debt, or living paycheck to paycheck; if each year resembles the year before; if the challenges in your life are not of your own choosing; if they arrive as minor problems that are the result of neglect, then this strategy is absolutely necessary for your growth and fulfillment: Set worthy challenges! Challenge yourself to get in the best shape of your life, to run a marathon, to lose twenty-five or fifty pounds, to save twenty percent of your income, to launch your own business, to follow your dreams, whatever they may be. It can be done; people do it every day. Challenge yourself with giant financial goals. If these financial goals inspire you to cut your expenses, to dream up new sources of income, then fantastic. Challenge yourself to learn a new skill, to travel to a faraway place, to build a charitable foundation, to pay off your mortgage in ten years or less. Then, go to work. Read the books, do the exercises, practice the daily success habits in this book, and become more than you ever imagined. This book gives you the resources, but the accelerant, the jet fuel, is the challenge, and the engine resides in you. Capacity is only a state of mind. Set a big challenge now. Tell the person closest to you, put everything on the line, and put all that you have into it. This is the Warrior of Life way.

Chapter Summary:

People who are succeeding in life do things differently from those who are struggling. They allocate their time towards high value activities. They recognize the importance of tending to their own needs, and developing their own potential, so they take actions on these every day. Average people, on the other hand, spend much of their time on things that don't matter and never have time for the things, which matter most which can make all the difference. For example, reading, versus watching mindless TV, and exercising in the morning, instead of sleeping in, are just two areas that can have a major positive impact on a person's life. The key is to consciously put those practices in place each day until they have become natural habits. Use the suggestions in this chapter to help you schedule those things – Daily Success Habits – that can make all the difference in your life.

Next, it wasn't until I started studying success and interviewing successful individuals that I realized, how almost all of them set big goals and take on large challenges. In fact, the willingness to embrace challenges appears to be a common fabric connecting successful people from all walks of life, together. The average person, on the other hand, typically, avoids potential challenges like the plague. They never recognize that actively pursuing worthwhile goals, whose achievement lies just on the other side of a major challenge, is the key to extracting all the positive aspects of life. Just as a muscle grows from increased resistance, and coal is converted to a diamond due to intense pressure, our potential is released by taking on difficult challenges, which force us to expand our capacity. By embracing challenges and then reframing them in your mind, by applying the techniques previously discussed in this book, such as *solution thinking* and *inverse thinking*, you are positioning yourself to manifest the life of your dreams.

Action Steps:

1. Commit yourself to making the Daily Success Habits explained in this chapter a regular part of your day.

2. Identify areas where you have been playing small, and commit yourself to setting larger goals and taking on greater challenges.

3. Examine the things in your life that you may have been procrastinating on. Determine an action plan to complete them, immediately. If it is a large project, apply Kaizen, and break it down into smaller steps.

4. Look for challenges in your workplace, and begin trying to identify solutions. Use the power of posing challenges as questions, to invoke the aid of your subconscious mind. Read each question, and identify twenty possible solutions.

Chapter 10

Living a Life of Purpose

As I've already written, when I was kid, like most kids I wanted to be a superhero. Unlike most kids, I didn't let this dream fade, as I got older. I realized that it probably wasn't realistic for me to put on a costume and run around town fighting crime (although, as I write this, there are groups of people across the country doing that very thing; Google the name "Phoenix Jones"). However, I was still committed to making a positive difference in the lives of many, both professionally and personally. I looked for ways to contribute to my community, and, in doing so, stumbled upon one of the greatest secrets of happiness in the world, which is doing good for others. Contributing to the welfare of others through charitable activities, community service, and giving, is one of the fastest ways to enjoy the highest emotions of peace of mind, love, appreciation, and gratitude. Emerson says, "To know that one life has breathed easier because you have lived. This is to have succeeded." So, imagine the level of life success you'll get to enjoy, when you are a contributing factor in helping, many, lives to breathe easier.

Volunteering, giving, and contributing to the well-being of others is easy to do; of course, it's, also, easy not to. So many people get caught up in their own trivial problems, and the mundane details of their own lives, that they never take the time to make any difference in the lives of people who are really suffering and are in need. The paradox I found, in my own life, was that, the more I have ever given of myself and of my resources to others, the more good things which have shown up in my life. I believe that this is one of the magical laws of the Universe: the more you give, the more you get. (What a wonderful Universe.) Unfortunately, too many people don't get much out of life, because they don't give much. Don't let this be you.

Give

I was first introduced to the joy of giving as a young man, not even realizing the portent of what I was endeavoring to do. When I was in college, each day, while driving to classes, I would take a short cut through the housing projects in New Haven. I would often see kids hanging around on the sidewalks and corners as I drove by, and this got me thinking. I thought of how fortunate I had been to learn the martial arts, and what a difference it could make for these children as well. I realized that for most of them, enrolling in a martial arts school might be a luxury that their parents couldn't quite afford. This bothered me, and, each day, as I drove to school, I thought more and more about it; little did I know that, subconsciously, an idea was forming. Soon, I was imagining the difference I could make if I had the opportunity to share these gifts I had received – the martial arts training – with the kids of this community. I saw myself, in my mind's eye, teaching a weekly class in a courtyard, in the center of the housing projects. By that time in my life, I had already read at least fifty to a hundred self-growth books, and I knew that the best time to act on an idea was when the "idea was fresh and the inspiration high." So, with a little research and a lot of tenacity, I was eventually introduced to the head of the community affairs, for that part of the city of New Haven. During a meeting with him in his office, I told him what I wanted to do, and after he was done laughing, he told me, it wouldn't be possible, because of the potential liability. Not to be deterred, I started focusing on a possible solution, only to find that the solution was right beneath my feet. At that time I was teaching a regular martial arts program at the Valley YMCA, in Ansonia, CT, and I decided to request the use of the facility for my program. I would donate my time, every week, for a year, and the YMCA would donate the use of the training room for two hours, every Saturday, for a year, to which they agreed. I, then, began to design my class. As I wrote earlier, I wanted this class to be a vehicle for the participants, not only to learn self-defense, but, also, to learn life skills, such as the ones I had been learning in the books I was reading. I wanted to create young Warriors of Life, individuals who would live by a code of ethics, who would develop their character, and who would know how to access their own mental resources to achieve their goals. I wanted to create Warriors who would succeed on the battlefield of life.

Thus, the first incarnation of the Warrior of Life class was born. Almost immediately, the class gained local publicity, being featured on the front page of the community section of the regional newspaper on Christmas Day. Children flocked to my class. Parents thanked me for the good I was doing which inspired me to do more. In fact, I still maintain a relationship with a handful of the students in that class, so many years later.

As I mentioned before, once you begin doing things to help others, the Universe responds by doing things for you, and the rewards from that first class continue to come to me, as well. Warrior of Life has evolved, from a weekly class for kids, to a philosophy for living and succeeding, which I have used and shared with many others over the years. Next, it became an Adult Community Education class, then, weekend seminars, and, currently, this book. Plus, a portion of the proceeds of this book will go to supporting foundations that embody the Warrior of Life philosophy, foundations which are committed to teaching individuals life skills and providing them with resources to apply those skills in the marketplace. (Also a portion will be designated to students as scholarships for college.)

Marjorie's Story

One such organization this book will support is Dress for Success. I first read about Dress for Success many years ago in Richard Carlson's great little book, "Don't Sweat the Small Stuff." I did a quick search on the internet, and I found that there was a Dress for Success location nearby. I contacted the Executive Director and offered to volunteer to teach individuals how to find a job and advance their career, to which I was welcomed. So, one day each week, I would go with Marjorie McAllister, the Community Development Director, and we would teach a one and a half hour course on career development at the Department of Labor. While volunteering there, I came to learn a little of Marjorie's story. She had actually been a client of Dress for Success. She arrived there, lacking confidence, shy, and withdrawn. She had found herself in a difficult situation and Dress for Success (DFS) provided the *vehicle* for her to grow and improve. She became a part of the Professional Women's Group, which met each month to teach new skills and develop its clients. Eventually Marjorie was able to build her confidence, and she began speaking about DFS, around the community. Audience members were, naturally, moved after hearing her story, and the reach of DFS grew, through her efforts. This turned into a professional paid role for her, working directly for the Fairfield County chapter of DFS. When I began working with Marjorie, she had been recently chosen to study in a professional development program at Yale; she had her own radio show; she worked in the community for DFS, and she, also, volunteered regularly for a number of organizations. She is an example of setting challenging goals and seeking to make a measurable difference in the lives of many. She embodies the Warrior of Life philosophies of using available resources to improve and, then, from a position of success, to endeavor to give back in different ways.

This, by the way, is the message I would share with attendees of our class at the Department of Labor. Many of them were in the class because they had been out of work for upwards of two years. Many had other challenges they were facing, as well. As part of the total message that we would share with them, I would tell them to identify resources, such as the free business attire provided by DFS, and to make use of those resources to achieve their goals, such as finding gainful employment. Then I would talk about the next part of the formula, which was, once they had achieved the results, and things were improving, to commit themselves to giving back, through volunteering and donations of time and resources, to help other people in need. After they found jobs, how many people do you think accepted my challenge and decided to give back? The budding Warriors of Life did, I am sure, and I am certain those who are giving back are continuing to grow and succeed in their own lives.

Soup Kitchen

After launching the Warrior of Life class, and well before volunteering for DFS, I expanded my list of volunteer initiatives. I began volunteering at a soup kitchen in New Haven. Every Friday, I would report to a church in New Haven, which was in the area near Yale, and it was a part of the Downtown Evening Soup Kitchen organization (DESK). There, in the church basement, I would help to feed sixty to seventy people, many who were homeless or in dire straits. This led me to get involved in coat drives and other activities, which I still do to this day. I was so enjoying helping others, that I started to feel like a real superhero, and this motivated me to do more. Plus, as I already mentioned, the more I would give, the more I would receive in personal benefits, above and beyond the tremendous satisfaction I was gaining and above and beyond the feeling that I was making a difference. At the DESK soup kitchen for example, many of the other volunteers were either current students or graduates of Yale. Though the soup kitchen, my network expanded to now include many successful individuals, and they in turn introduced me to many beneficial opportunities, all because I walked through the open door of volunteering.

You Can Make a Difference

The purpose of these examples is to inspire you to combine the strategy, presented in the last chapter, setting audacious challenges for yourself, with the strategy in this chapter, to live a life of real value, by helping all of those in need, throughout your community and the world. This is the essence of being a Warrior of Life, cultivating a strong character, living a life of power, and making a positive difference in the world. Making a difference is part and parcel of what all of the masters have done. Look at Gandhi for example. He started out as a lawyer. He recognized the injustice taking place around him, and he committed himself to the daunting challenge of gaining freedom, peacefully, for the people of India. To accomplish this, he developed his mind and his spirit. He disciplined himself, he tested himself, and he put forth massive effort, and, in the end, he was successful. Be like Gandhi, in your own life. Set large challenges for yourself, use this book to build your mental, spiritual, and physical foundation, and, then, make a difference in the world. Start by helping just one life to breathe easier, and let it gain *momentum*.

My final lesson to you in this book, to which this entire chapter is devoted, is to inspire you to make the commitment, and to take action by leveraging your personal resources, to make an even larger difference in the world. In a great book, one I've already recommended called *The Seven Habits of Highly Effective People*, Stephen Covey talks about the importance of leaving a legacy. Similarly, Robin Sharma, one of North America's most popular leadership speakers suggests you ask yourself the question, "Who will cry when you die?" Both authors understand that there is much to gain by devoting yourself to something larger than the daily details of your own life.

I believe the real purpose of every individual life on this planet is to help another. We all are part of the Universal family, and we were designed to take care of our brethren. You will find the most success in all areas of your life, and the greatest fulfillment, when you commit a part of your life to making a difference in the lives of others. As a Warrior of Life, by practicing everything you have learned in this book, you are now equipping yourself to help those in need, to stand up for those who can't defend themselves, and to contribute greatly to all of mankind. If you persist in achieving large challenges for yourself and always work to make a difference, yours will be an exceptional life. You will be a real superhero for yourself, to your family, and in your community.

How to Begin

In Stephen Covey's book, he suggests that you, "Begin with the end in mind," and another way to do that is to imagine your obituary. How would you want it to read? Along with this, imagine you have lived a long, prosperous life, it's your funeral, and the place is packed. People are lined up, out the door, to pay their respects to you and to eulogize your contribution to them, and to the world. What will they say about you? What would you like them to say? Perhaps, someone will say how, every year, you organized a coat drive at your office, how you involved the adjacent offices to participate, and how, thanks to you, people, less fortunate, were able to keep warm. Or perhaps an adult will get up to say how, when he was a child, you would come to his school, each week, and mentor him making a positive difference in his life. Perhaps, someone will say how you volunteered at a soup kitchen and always went out of your way to make everyone feel special. Or, perhaps, the executive director of a local charitable organization will have you to thank, for leading the campaign to raise money for the building they now occupy.

Most likely they will speak, not only of the many things you did, but, also, of the things you stood for, as well. What do you want to be remembered for? What values do you stand for and refuse to compromise? How are you living out these values in your life? One of the values I live for is, equality for all. I abhor racism in any form. If I see anyone treated unfairly, I make it a point to do something about it. How about you? What are you willing to stand up for?

Lastly, I often hope that at my funeral, or in my obituary, one of the things that will be said is, "What he wanted for himself, he wanted for everyone, and, whenever he found something good, he would share it." That is the purpose of this book. What you hold in your hands is some of the best ideas, strategies, and philosophies for successful living which I have found, so far. May they help you to make a difference, in your own life, as they have done in mine!

Action Steps:

1. Imagine your funeral. What would you want people to say about you? Write it down.
2. Write your obituary. List the values you stand for. Are you living them each day?
3. Identify places in your community, where you can volunteer. Gain momentum by taking action.
4. Before you go to sleep each night, ask yourself, "Have more lives breathed easier because I have lived?"

Conclusion

Give yourself a destiny to live up to.

Throughout history, a common belief, held by an uncommon few, those Warriors of Life who dared to change the world and succeeded, has been the belief in their own magnificent destiny. Alexander the Great was told repeatedly, by his mother, from a very young age, that he was destined for greatness, and he went on to build the world's largest empire. Gandhi was a believer in destiny. He is quoted as speaking about how an individual creates his own destiny, through his values and character; he also believed in the destiny of India. His role in manifesting that destiny impacted the entire nation. John D. Rockefeller believed it was his chosen destiny to amass a fortune and, then, to distribute it, in the name of God, to worthy causes. This belief inspired him to build the largest business concern, at that time, in history, amassing a fortune, which, in his later years, he worked tirelessly to distribute. Athletes, business tycoons, philanthropists, and leaders, from all walks of life, when analyzed closely, can be found to possess *a belief in their own destiny for success.*

A warrior and the concept of destiny go hand in hand, and if you desire to become someone of significance and success, giving yourself a magnificent destiny to live up to, is a surefire way to inspire yourself to succeed. Begin by asking the question: What will be my destiny? Then, supply the answer of your choosing.

Will your destiny be to feed multitudes of people, to be a fair and just employer of many, to amass a fortune, to save lives, to make a difference in your community and in the lives of people you care about, or to defend your country and its values? Is it your destiny to raise a wildly successful family, to travel the world exploring its mysteries, to be a voice for those who can't defend themselves, to organize your community, to stand up for what's noble? Whatever your dreams, ignite them with the belief in your own significant destiny.

This book is your guide along the road to your destiny. Regularly, go to the Goal Setting Workshop detailed in chapter six and utilize it to continue to shape your life, by formulating your specific goals and developing plans to manifest them. If you run into any problems along the way, chapter five will remind you how to apply "solution thinking" to reframe those difficulties and overcome them. Does your destiny require you to stretch beyond your comfort zone? Well, chapter three has taught you how, immediately, to adopt the characteristics of someone who can rise above any obstacle. If you continue to follow the suggestions in chapter eight, you will strengthen your body for the journey; and, chapter nine will help you to keep your priorities in tow each day, as you prepare to tackle the major challenges that will lift you to the level of success you desire. Chapter ten will help you remember why you are doing it all and what this life is really all about – "becoming more through helping others."

This book has been written plainly, each sentence carefully chosen to impart the greatest amount of knowledge in the most succinct manner possible. I've endeavored to include as many practical ideas, techniques, principles, and strategies as possible to help you progress swiftly towards your goals. Read this book often, make it one of your few Warrior of Life possessions, along with your journal, that you keep nearby as your advance in the direction of your dreams and manifest your destiny.

About the Author

Chuck Householder is a dynamic professional speaker and trainer, who speaks to companies of all sizes, sharing with them his unique philosophy on personal achievement and success. In addition to keynote speeches centered on the concepts presented in this book, his company Charles Householder Enterprises offers comprehensive sales training programs to consumer and B2B sales organizations. His program Selling on the Extra Mile has grown increasingly popular; as a result he recently recorded it in audio format so sales professionals can listen to it, again and again, at their desks and in their automobiles. Householder is currently writing a book based on this program.

To hire Chuck Householder to speak at your company, school, trade association, church, civic organization, or event, please visit http://www.charleshouseholder.com for contact information.

CPSIA information can be obtained at www.ICGtesting.com
Printed in the USA
LVOW082113150413

329247LV00001B/435/P